Living
On The Up High, Not The Down Low©

The Movement To Uplift Good Black Men and the Empowerment of the African American Family

Aaron Anwar Smith

To My Dearest Cousin
To Cha Cha,

Thank you so much for your Love & Support!
May Happiness and success cloud your
Days & Bring Joyous Rain

Love,

Living
On The Up High,
Not The Down Low©

For information, contact:
The Up High Association,
P.O. Box 55163
Washington, DC, 20040

www.OnTheUpHigh.com

For worldwide distribution.

ISBN: 978-0-9795-0650-5
LCCN: 2007931553

Printed in the United States of America
Signature Book Printing, www.sbpbooks.com

Photography By
James C. Jackson & Rajesh Nair

Cover design by
Lori A. Fields www.vcas.design.com

God,

Grant me the serenity to accept the things I cannot change, the courage to change the things I can, and the wisdom to know the difference.

Amen.

www.OnTheUpHigh.com

To all who struggle and strive to stay on the straight, narrow road leading to righteousness; you are so few, but serve as examples for so many.

CONTENTS

www.OnTheUpHigh.com

Introduction

"Where in the world are all of the good Black men? Are they in jail, dead, or gay? Why are there so few within professional environments? Why are there so many more Baby's Daddies than there are husbands? Why is the college enrollment of Black men so much lower than Black women? What is the deal with men being on the down low? What are the real issues that are affecting the Black family and community?"

The above questions have plagued our lives, offices, homes, barbershops, beauty salons, and churches for too long. Until now, we have walked down many endless corridors searching for the answers to these questions that seem to elude the grasps of the people who have asked them. Until now, the man living on the up high has been silent, but will be silent no more.

Living On the Up High was written from the view point of African American males and females who, at some point, noticed a dire need to close the relational gap between them. The long awaited answers to questions many women have asked now bring much light to many significant topics amongst Black people today. This tool will provide you with those answers and help you find your own.

What Is Living On the Up High?

Living On the Up High references a principle set by positive, honest men who value positive, heterosexual relationships. In our society, the label represents Black men who make every attempt to uplift themselves, their families, and their communities. This standard opposes the 'Down Low' man's reality, which was explained by Mr. J.L. King in his book *On the Down Low*. Men on the 'Up High', however, live their lives honorably, through God with determination, strength, and integrity. They stand out by using that strength and walking forthright while exercising wisdom to guide them along the way.

The down low term, on the other hand, represents men who cheat on their women with men. These men are shameful individuals who feel the need to hide from reality in order to feel fulfilled and satisfied. On the other hand, men who live Up High feel no desire to hide from themselves, because they have nothing to be ashamed of. To them, living a down low or low down existence is not an option.

Living on the Up High means living with values widely upheld by Black men everywhere. This goal is set and reached by the man who lives life for himself, his family, and God. An Up High man values his interactions with others and works diligently to make every action and behavior the best possible. He loves his Black woman and proves it daily. Ironically, however, many do not believe that these actions confirm a man's Up High status, and to that I say, "To each his or her own," but I can guarantee that if those people tried living their lives this way, their doubts would disappear.

From a spiritual aspect, it should be known that this vehicle for righteousness should always be used with God as the focal point. After all, Up High without God is truly down low, and we all know that we do not want to go down there.

Another interesting fact about the Up High standard is that it does not just promote a better quality of life for the male gender. Women who value enlightenment and venerability also live Up High lives. From sisters who are the most important link in the family chain, to strong single mothers struggling for daily success by themselves, I celebrate you. Without you, there would be no *we*, and need *we* because *I* can't change things alone.

Aside from all of the other positive references of this book, *Living On the Up High's* message works at a relentless pace to dispel the myth of there being little to no good Black men left in this country. I will show you this through the use of realistic examples and rational reasons displaying why some would believe the hurtful criticisms, rumors, and inequities normally found within the production of mainstream media and society. The Up High message serves as a guide to reconnect Black heterosexual relationships in addition to a being a psych-sociological survey of the ideas and mindsets of men and women who share different experiences and opinions about the successes and failures of Black heterosexual relationships.

Your Journey To Up Highness

While traveling through this Up High experience, take note of the emphasis I place on the knowledge and recognition of African American history, along with the senses of strength, resiliency, and forgiveness this book presents. I use our true African American history as the foundation so we all may see and recognize how the effects of our pasts hinder us today. It is essential that we acknowledge and grasp that understanding so we can move forward together. All of these topics should be studied and used as mechanisms to help us define ourselves as opposed to allowing others do it for us. We can and will ultimately gain control over the weapons that deploy evil images of our people into our own minds and into the minds of others.

The journey for Black men and women has seemed like an unending emotional roller coaster, leading us up and down on a dark and narrow track. It is now time for us to get out of the car, realize who put us on the track, and step off of it to get our homes in order.

This book should be used as a device to repair the rift between African American women and men, and should also be used to dispel stereotypes that have been driven into our very being. It will help you form your own opinions and motivate you to think about why things are the way that they are today. I also anticipate that your present view of yourself and others will also be challenged in your reading, so prepare yourself for a mental makeover.

On a personal note, I would like for you to place as much emotion into this book as I have. During your journey, prepare to laugh, cry, shout out obscenities, yell thanksgiving praises, and nod your head in agreement when you see yourself or someone you know within the pages of this book.

A Little About Me

Some readers may wonder what made me decide to stand up in defense of good Black men, regarding the creation of this book, and that is fine. That is exactly what I want you to do. Please question me. I want you to be intrigued by my presence, challenge my opinions in addition to your own, because I want you to think about your individual growth, which you can use to help others. This book will make a difference in someone's life. I know this because it is through the will of God that I began this project, and all things through Him do prosper.

There are many people who preach and write books that explain what we need to do to come together as a people, and I thank God for each and every one of them. They do things like discuss topics dealing with such issues as past church influences in Black communities in addition to the church's community involvement and its ability to turn things around. I support issues like these, but I have an idea that can help as well.

I believe that we should start from our roots and place good, progressive strategies at the beginning of our relationships. Think about it from nature's perspective. All roots were once seeds. If we could successfully plant the seeds of divine righteousness and relationship into our own minds, our roots would then recreate the strong foundation that we need to stand strong together. This idea is like that of an investment. If the power of God and a positive family atmosphere were what our children were raised believing in, the next generation would be far more successful than our present generation of our youth. Imagine what kind of power they would have if they were taught correctly. They would not be seeds anymore; they would be known as the fruitful product of a beautiful race that loves each of its own unconditionally.

In explanation of my purpose, I did not believe I had to obtain a Doctorate in philosophy or any other type of scholarly study in order to create this book about the empowerment of African American culture and loving relationships. I merely wanted to present my experiences and the experiences of others for the purpose of opening a few eyes. In addition, I would like this book to help you and others think about the way you do things. Most of all, I want you to ask yourself if you are doing everything you can to improve yourself for you, your lover, and your people. If your answers are yes, yes, and yes, then you are on your way. Lastly, while reading, I want you to be able to recognize key factors that may lead you to reasons why you may think the way you do about other African Americans. Whatever feeling those emotions project is fine. Ultimately, my goal is to help you become aware of your reality and base your decisions on it.

What I Want From You

I accept the fact that you may disagree with my personal opinions on certain topics. To me, that reality is totally adequate. When you do disagree though, I would like for you to substitute my opinions with those of your own, from a realistic stance of course. With regard to your analysis of the situation between African American men and women, please consider all possibilities and not just the ones in front of your face. In addition, after reading this book, I want you to motivate yourself and others to begin initiating actions that will ultimately and effectively help empower African American Relationships and marriages, which will ultimately secure our future.

Take time to look deep inside yourself, during and after your reading, and focus on your knowledge of the issues at hand. Understand and teach others by correcting their notions of identifying with destructively used terms that are not synonymous with African Americanism such as, *ghetto* and *down low*. It is urgent that you and I define our own existence and create a unified understanding of who we are.

On this day, I have been graced with God's direction and have chosen to accept my calling. I do this because I love you, and I refuse to be silent about it anymore. I hope you enjoy!

One

Our African History In America

Why We Must Know It

Without knowledge of our history, we are nowhere, and we are nobody.

When referring to a culture of people, one must understand how important the role of history is for that culture's existence. That same recognition is needed to understand how African American history has been consistently altered, hidden, and lied about for so long in addition to how the effects have become devastatingly catastrophic. Because of this catastrophe, we Blacks must take the necessary actions to educate and train our people to think from historical and realistic perspectives so we can become better prepared for the future.

Through your analysis of the past, please do not place the blame of the many afflictions that African American people have experienced onto anyone. Try making an attempt to direct the focus of your historical views inward so questions can be answered, riddles solved, and myths expelled. I seek the truth and I implore you to do so as well.

Because history is the path to truth and understanding, we must remove the barriers and roughage that conceal the truth. We must do more than point out the evils that others place on us. We must overcome those evils. Only then will our minds be enlightened enough to understand and move past the issues that we have as African Americans.

This chapter will help you gain a clear view of why society views African Americans the way it does. On top of that, it should provide you with answers to the questions many people ask regarding the Black man's so called whereabouts, along with the answer to why people feel the need to ask in the first place.

I urge you to learn all about Black history by searching for answers that you are not aware of. This, in theory, will give you the deep satisfaction of realizing how great and strong our forbearers were and it will help you appreciate how important we are to one another. This is a challenge from me to you, as well as to myself because one thing is for certain: if we do not learn from our history, all of the contributions of our forefathers will be lost forever.

There is much information pertaining to our past that we are not knowledgeable about. What we need to do is go and find it. "Ask and it shall be given unto to you; seek and ye shall find." *Mathew 7:7* is the Bible verse that points toward the path on which our answers lie. Will you answer the challenge?

Black In the Day

I was not around during segregation, which ended in the 1960s, but I am aware of the realities of those times. Blacks during that era and before had a passionate love for one another that one could sense from a great distance. During those times they supported, motivated, and appreciated each other. We once loved and depended on each other and were unified groups and communities of people, who had the same interests and needs in mind. Somehow, we have become separate. Where we once communicated our joys and sorrows together, there is now an empty brokenness with little communication and understanding. Because of this, less and less of our men and women marry.

Question: Is our combined support of the political realm bringing us justice? My opinion is that the lack of our collective voting numbers and continued, heinous killing of one another, both oppose the reasons for our fight against the majority power, taking place during the period of desegregation. Voting, at that time, was not a personal privilege denied to one Black person. It was a civil right that was denied to all Blacks, so how could any African American person, today, not vote because he or she 'doesn't feel like it?' How can that person be so selfishly ungrateful and simultaneously remain sensitive to the beliefs of his or her elders who fought and died to give him or her proper justice? I have spoken with Black women and men alike, about the relational situation of Black people and have received consistent responses such as, "It ain't my problem, what's in it for me, and ain't nothing gonna ever change." "Where is the compassion for yourself and your own people?" I asked each of those who responded. The buck does not stop there though. I even ask myself questions about this issue at times, to make sure I am on the right track, and I encourage everyone to do the same.

We must, as a people, open our eyes and take a look around. One of the major reasons why we remain in our current state is because we do not seek out correct information like we should. Our unified level of literacy is not sufficient. Even though the enlightenment of many Blacks has delivered some success, we have not collectively taken advantage.

A relative fact referencing slavery is that there were certain laws in place that were designed to crush the Black race. The creators of those laws and codes knew that reading possessed the key to freedom, so they took that freedom away by making it impossible for Blacks to read legally. Now that we legally possess the tool of literacy, it is unbelievable that we are not using it to its fullest capacity.

The irony of this situation is painfully obvious, however, we must understand that we cannot succeed by holding anger against today's majority race. We simply will not get anywhere together by doing little to step toward the advancement of our progression if we keep placing so much emphasis on blaming Whites for all of our troubles. All this does is overshadow the journey to our goal. Instead, we would be so much better off if we used that energy for constructive purposes.

No one can keep or hide anything from us in books anymore. If we really want to find answers we will put forth the necessary effort to find those answers. That is the bottom line.

The Truth About Our History

It is well known that we have been lied to and misled from the very beginning. It is also widely known that the act of misleading any group of people, when referring to their historical heritage and culture, produces devastating results and consequences. This is not the way history should be used. History should be used as a tool to let people know who they are, where they are, and who they once were as well as where they should be. If history failed to do these things, then it would be of no use to any of us.

Legacy, on the other hand, is something that should be embraced and kept as it is passed through the generations. No people should ever be denied their legacy. Let me remind you that Africans were the only group of people who were robbed of theirs and forced to come to America against their will. They were dehumanized, stripped of their names, robbed of their history, and left to suffer. An unimaginable amount of legacies were destroyed. Many people do not know this because history, in America has not been taught truthfully. Do you know your history? Lets find out.

How familiar are you with the history of your people? Let's take a little quiz to see how much you know about your heritage.

•How many African American inventors, Scientists, or Civil Rights leaders of the past can you name off hand?

•What are the levels of entrepreneurship and ownership like for African Americans now, compared to that of forty years ago?

•How much appreciation or recognition have Blacks ever received for building this country during and after slavery?

You may or may not have answers to questions like these because the answers have purposely been delivered to us dishonestly, and have been hidden.

In addition to the concealment of Black accomplishment, today's power entities won't admit to or apologize for the inhumane treatment that Blacks have received since this country's pre-existence, but they will easily have you believe that George Washington never told a lie, and that Columbus discovered America, while helping the Natives achieve their fullest *'civilized'* potential. Most will even have you believe that Lincoln freed the slaves for their welfare. This is why knowing your history is important. You need to be able to weed out the lies and deception.

Misconceptions like these also lead us to believe many things about ourselves that just aren't true; like when former Mississippi Senator, Theodore Bilbo wrote, "Race is America's biggest problem," in his effort to have Negroes shipped back to Africa. I don't know how that sounds to you, but he seems to have believed that Blacks were to blame for America's problems. To go on, the majority powers of this country have even stooped so low as to compare and teach that the Holocaust created a more devastating experience for its victims than that of African slavery.

Why? Why would someone want to downgrade the result of more than four hundred years of slavery by attempting to place the suffering of the Holocaust above it? Some Jews even make it a point to push this argument, but why? I don't ever recall hearing Blacks advising any person of the Jewish faith to stop crying about racism when they were spat on by the entire world. Now they turn their backs on Blacks. Why is that so?

History goes on to show that the early Jewish population that migrated to America many years ago, suffered immensely during their settlement. They were treated like heathens and became inhabitants of what were originally known, in Germany, as ghettos. Did you know that? Look it up. The truth is out there. The expression ghetto, in America, has become a term that is somehow only related to Black people. There is poverty in Chinese, Jewish, and Irish towns all across America, but a person somehow has to visit a Black community to see a Ghetto. How is that so, when the term was created in Germany for Jews? Is it because the leaders of our country look at Blacks the same way Hitler and his followers viewed the Jews many years ago? It is very possible.

I personally have great sympathy for the Jews who were affected during and after the holocaust, but the positive thing about their transition was that they were accepted into the White race over time. That process, in comparison to many other ethnic groups, was easier by far for Jews, because of their skin tone and finances. Even though they were of a foreign ethnicity, the color of their skin granted them access to American favor.

The interesting, underlying point here is that Blacks could not cut off their skin to help them blend into mainstream society like the Jews did with their last names. Even if they wanted to, which they don't, they could not hide the beautiful hue of their physical essence.

I believe it is undeniably evident how certain cultures within the boundaries of our country would have us hate, disrespect, and kill our own, while disgracing our heritage for their amusement. I say this realizing that at every turn, Blacks are urged to remember the hardships and the oppressions of other cultures. We are pushed to commemorate the Holocaust, remember the Alamo, and celebrate Christopher Columbus' bogus discovery of the Americas, but we are always urged to forget about slavery. Why is that? Our adversaries are so quick to say to us, "Just let it go." "Slavery is over, stop pulling the race card." They even have the audacity to suggest, "Racism does not exist." Interesting, isn't it?

The fact of the matter is that many members of the majority race never wanted Blacks to succeed as a people from the beginning. They never wanted the beautiful men and women of our race to know that they were intelligent and strong. Those people were, and still remain as masters of lies and deception. Why else would they try to hinder our knowledge by not allowing us to read? Why else would they try to take away our freedom of speech by way of fire hoses and attack dogs? Why else would Blacks be denied reparations? Need I even bring up the devastation that was caused, not by hurricane Katrina, but by the weak, negligent response from the government?

The American racial dilemma of a half-century ago has been much eased, but a large inequality between young Black and White males still exists. We should not blame each other today, as men and women, because we did not cause any of this to occur. We should, however, reflect and really think about the reasons why we have the social issues that we battle with as a people. That is the key to understanding. We must also not play into the idea that racism is dead. Most of the same people who threw rocks at us, spat on us, hung us, and called us *niggers* are still alive today. We must not forget that. I am not suggesting that you or anyone else remember this for the purpose of rebellion. It is simply that we should know who and what we are really up against. Awareness is the key and I want you to use it to open the door to understanding and reality. Our color and heritage are not our enemies. They are our blessings.

Face It, Black Is Not black

When it comes to defining or labeling ourselves, color has been the issue for some time in this country. Who is white, and who is black? It almost seems that there are two teams trying to win a game by claiming as many colors as they can. Imagine, if you will, a boxing ring with an announcer screaming: "In the white corner we have Caucasians, Europeans, White Australians, South Americans, and other very light skinned ethnic groups." "And in the black corner we have African Americans, Black Africans, and Native Americans, Hispanics, Dominicans, and Haitians etc…" "We can't forget Black Europeans, and let's also throw Vin Diesel, The Rock, Lenny Kravitz, Tiger, and Mariah into the picture as toss ups.

I know this is not actually a game or match, but I'll be damned if it doesn't feel like it. It seems as though whoever has questionable skin tone and is in the spotlight is up for grabs, but this situation is bigger than any sports competition. It is the race of the races and the battle is over whose skin (spirit) is the most pure.

When it comes to being questionably colored or partially pure, I'm sure that significantly fair skinned people get grilled consistently about their racial background. They probably grow up with all types of identity crisis issues that trouble them into adulthood. My argument is simple but straight to the point. I believe that people are not born black or white. Every single person in the world is colored. What is the big misunderstanding? This is the only nation where the terms 'black' and 'white' are used, solely, for the purpose of classification. I guarantee that if you ask a German immigrant, who has been in America for one day, if he is White, he will reply, "No. I am German." This is generally the same way of thinking for most foreign immigrants, until they learn the ways of this American society. Dr. Claude Anderson, the author of the highly influential book *Powernomics*, hinted to this idea by explaining how after a few weeks of living in America, a person who has immigrated will usually have noticed our nation's problems with racial disparity. My opinion is that it's just an act of picking sides. He goes on to explain how the ones who favor the Caucasian persuasion quickly form into their shared groups, comprised of the majority race and its feeder, immigrant societies, and how they shut Blacks out of the economical and political economic marketplace. Like I said, "It's just an act of picking sides."

The terrible effects that stem from the energy of misunderstood notions and assumptions are the reason why this chapter is so important. I have a strong belief that we should all understand and recognize the reasons for the subliminal conditioning that has taken place in America and the world. There are certain physical powers that view Blacks with great disdain. They have designed an invisible machine to ensure the destruction of Black Americans and have manipulated this country in a way that has convinced members of other cultures to pin negativity onto Blackness. They want every race to ultimately look down on Blacks with a certain level of condescension. In addition, they designed their machine to manipulate our minds into disliking our own skin color and culture. Because this is so, I have made it my duty to help you and others realize these truths and recognize this pattern, so you can locate within yourself, any unnoticeable, self-destructive habits that you may have towards your being and your people.

Open your eyes and begin your recovery from the effects of the every day trance that our societal negativity has us stuck in. Do not be ashamed of your African lineage or your skin tone. As a matter of fact, there's nothing else you should rather be.

The Label Game

For Blacks, it has been an interesting journey, while shifting our descriptive title from African to African American. These sequences have shown me how our self-defining methods to produce labels for our culture and ourselves have become inadequate. I believe that we need to create a name that defines us completely. As far as the way we have labeled ourselves goes, I personally am not fully satisfied with what we have come up with thus far. First we were African, then Negro, Colored, Black, and lastly African American. The reasons why I do not support these labels 100% are because they do not solely define the experience or existence of my people. After viewing the pattern, it should become obvious to you as well.

In the late 1700s, free Blacks still referred to themselves as Africans. Though they felt their heritage slipping away, it was still important for them to continue with their traditions. However, those same traditions faded away because the Africans had no way of recording their history outside of stories and songs. Not being allowed to read, write, or even converse, at times, that option faded.

Slavery continued to deteriorate the people, yet the fact that remained was that they were still African and carried their name proudly. Evidence of this is shown through the creation of the African Methodist Episcopal Church (AME) in 1794. This Christian denomination was designed in an effort to worship God and to carry out the spirit of the original free African society. It was born through adversity, as a subdivision of the Methodist church. The reason for the split from the Methodist church was not as a result of differences between the two. It came to be so as a result of a time period, which was stamped by man's acts of illiberality against his fellow man by way of the color of his skin. Many of those un-Christian-like practices and ideas were brought into the church, which led Richard Allen along with others of color, to form an extended AME denomination.

After the emancipation of slaves, when African was no longer the preferred term of description, the once proclaimed Africans began using the terms Colored and Negro as terms of self-classification. They began to pull away from their African label, because they didn't believe that label pertained to them or their culture anymore. The incorporation of these new, defining terms in the once African community was looked at as a form of advancement for Blacks.

The National Association for the Advancement of Colored People (NAACP), an organization founded in 1909, is an example of the 'Colored' term usage in societal organizations existing during that time period. During those times, being Colored was something to honor and be proud of.

Black was the next widely used and accepted label of association for Colored people. It gained mass notoriety throughout the 1950s and 1960s, during the Civil Rights Movement when the new Black way of living and acceptance changed many things in America. It gave the people hope and made them proud to call themselves Black. They became encouraged and began to feel good about themselves. Statements like, "Black Power," and "I'm Black, and I'm proud," became encouraging symbols of hope and acted as vehicles of empowerment for all.

By the time the name 'African American' was born into our society, life had gotten a little better for Blacks. African Americans had forced their way into the sight of White America and began gaining more opportunities as a result. African American was selected as a term that introduced Blacks as the closest descendants of Africa, who lived in America. In reality the term does do that, but there are also some things it does not do. It does not give us a precise pointer to our being. In order for me to understand this concept on my own, I had to break things down. What do the terms African and American say about me? To some degree, I agree with general scientific theory that describes how humans were born from the region known today as Africa, also known as the cradle of civilization. In this case, we all should all carry some sort of reference of our African descent in our definitive descriptions of our own cultures. With this understanding, my question to my fellow Americans is, "What does Africa say about me that it doesn't say about you?" Does it make me less of a person to know that my ancestors left Africa a few hundred or thousand years after yours did? Why? If Africa is the motherland to us all, then why is everyone in such a rush to lose that connection? What is so evil about Africa that makes others want to renounce their ties to it?

Color Me Bad

Obvious facts show us that black and white are colors, simply put. There is not one person who can walk into a paint store, get samples of both colors, match the samples to their skin, and honestly say that they, themselves, are black or white. By the way, my skin tone is actually brown with a hinted hue similar to that of bronze. What color are you?

I appreciate knowing that there is more to the Black heritage than any color can define. There is great legacy behind the name. I love my people and because I do, I oppose this term. The obvious reality is that black is a color. That is all that needs to be said.

Our people were called Black long before we decided to accept the term in the 20th century, but my opinion is that we should not accept anything that has nothing to do with us. Just because we are accustomed to something, does not mean we have to permit it.

The term Negro follows the same concept. Do you really know what this word means? You'd be surprised at the amount of people who are not aware of the word's meaning or origin. Negro comes from the Latin root word *Niger*, which, in Latin, means black. The majority of the more popular spoken languages of the world are of Latin influence and use similar root bases. Take Spanish, for example. Within that language, negro means black (color). However, most American dictionaries will have you believe that Negro was a word created for us, by us. The website at www.dictionary.com displays its definition of Negro as follows: "*Negro – A Black person. A member of the Negroid race. Not in scientific use.*" Now if I am correct, someone out there marked us with the 'scientific' name Negroid, and then stated, "Not in scientific use." Make up your mind! First of all, what in the world is a Negroid? I am surely not a Negroid. Let's look a little deeper into this issue. *The American Heritage Book of English Usage* defines Negroid as follows: "*Negroid, one of the terms proposed by European anthropologists in the 18th and 19th centuries as part of a system of human racial classification. It refers to the indigenous peoples of Africa, south of the Sahara Desert. It is sometimes applied to certain peoples native to Indonesia, New Guinea, Melanesia, and the Philippines as well. In all cases it is now considered both out of date and likely to cause offense.*" They are damn right that it is likely to cause offense. It then goes on to describe other 'scientific' terms for different racial groups, by displaying names like Mongoloid, Caucasoid, and Australoid, in addition to stating how there is no such thing as a pure race in any meaningful sense." So if that is the case, what's the big fuss about? Why aren't we all friends, instead of enemies? Why can't we put our race issues behind us?

During the American period of slavery, and before accepting the term, enslaved Africans were referred to as Negro, which changed to

Nigger, because of southern dialect and mispronunciation. What they didn't realize was that both terms, being one in the same, always carried messages of ill intent. Later, the term 'Colored,' which defines itself and describes every person in the entire world, was also adopted. Around 1955, Negro leaders decided to change our label from Negro (*Nigger)* to Black, which means the exact same thing, *black*. Do you have your thinking cap on yet?

Years after integration, in 1989, another one of our beloved tiles was dropped yet again, only to bare birth to the new description of our heritage, namely, 'African American.' There are a few reasons why I, along with few others who share my thoughts, do not believe this term does us any justice. To me, these two words seem like they represent more people than I have the ability to identify with. Technically and genealogically speaking, the term 'African American' describes every single person in America. Since we all genealogically originated in Africa, and if we are American citizens, then we all are African American. If you only understand the usage of this term by the way the American standard has trained you to think about things then I can understand how it could be generally accepted as the term that defines Blacks. Most would say, "But you know what we mean when we use the term." Yes that is correct, but let's think outside of the box. We only understand the misrepresented meaning of this term because of how we manipulate its true definition. When African American was created, no one thought about the fact that color plays no part in the technical meaning of the term. Take a look at Africa, which is populated by both dark skinned African and Caucasian African inhabitants. For example, a Caucasian South African who is granted American citizenship would also be considered an African American. That person would then be eligible to receive specific benefits, scholarships, and quite honestly could become head of major African American organizations, without our best interest in mind. Sure, the likelihood of this happening is small, but my point is that 'African American' needs to be dropped just as the other terms were. I yearn for this to happen for the same reasons that the other incorrect names were dropped. They were replaced because they did not totally represent our heritage, nor did they represent us. Here is a question: Do dark skinned people living in England, who are closely related to Africa, refer to themselves as African British? I have never heard of that. The same goes for any other nation in the world.

I really want you to understand that I honor, promote, and cherish my heritage. My strongest desire is to bring its powerful past to the light of truth, but we must define ourselves correctly before we can successfully do that and stand in the light of our predecessors. Unfortunately, selecting a name that defines oneself along with millions of others isn't the easiest thing to do, but it can be done with unity. I do not believe that we, as African Americans, have succeeded in choosing the proper term of identification for ourselves. Each time that one of our selected terms of classification has been dropped, a more suitable one has been created, supposedly. We need to pick a meaningful name and stick with it. It is very important that we take the proper initiative in this effort because defining ourselves is the first step to knowing who we are and realizing our true abilities.

Furthermore, why do words like 'ghetto' and 'down low' only point toward African American environments? Why have only half of the people who have answered the question, "Do you know where the term ghetto comes from?" answered correctly? How can down low lifestyles be specific to Black men when White men carry the torch? The obvious fact is that there are more White men in America who marry women and romance men than there are Black down low men. How come they are not referred to as down low? Also, one does not hear much about White unfaithfulness, or Asians, who cheat on their spouses for that matter. Blacks seem to carry that burden for everyone somehow. The African American race is not a garbage heap that should stand for the rest of the nation dumping its crap onto Black heads.

I love my people and have pride for my legacy, and for that reason I want nothing but the best for all of us. If we are going to do anything at all, then let's do it to the fullest. I will not fill out optional forms urging me to check descriptions for myself that do not fit my belief. If I have to, I will make one up on my own, but I will not be misrepresented. I want whoever reads this book to think about that. Do your research and check things out on your own. You will learn a lot and want to pass that information along. These steps would help us feel better about ourselves as Blacks, and aid our healing process together, as men and women.

The Hidden Picture

When children are born, they don't automatically know that they want to attend Harvard University and major in physics. I say this to prove how everything that we know is either learned or created after we discover how to plan. In most cases, children are taught early, how to think and act.

Therefore, once the child naturally becomes mature enough to plan and make his own decisions, he naturally becomes drawn towards living out the values learned from his or her parents.

Sadly, too many circumstances outside of education point to the fact that too many children are being raised by television, which is especially bad for Black children. I say this because television, which is the main tool of American media, often presents distorted images of African Americans, which are very far from the truth. Those influences often do more damage than society cares to admit to. This concept should not be difficult for you to fathom because it has always been this way in America. I speak more about this topic in the chapter entitled, *The Woman's Point Of View*, where I reference the classic Sambo that served as a false visual misrepresentation of Blacks, in an effort to promote the laughter of whites. The goal at that time was to disempower Blacks by making them believe they were inferior. To this day, I believe that Black children and adults struggle, while sinking below their fullest potential, because of the after-effects of the institution of slavery that haunt us daily. This situation is similar to the reason why some Blacks don't vote. They just don't feel that it will make a difference and don't really believe that their side can win. A parallel reference can also be made to slavery and why many slaves never tried to escape. The people, in those cases, had their hope and pride stolen from them, which made them very dependent and hopeless. It is hard to believe and may not be as bad as it was then, but we are in a similar situation today.

My mother once asked me, at age five, what color I thought I was. I responded boldly, "I am White mommy." I thought this way because White was the only reference to heroism and greatness that I had, and I knew that I was going to be a hero. The Dukes of Hazzard was a show I loved to watch during that time. Those down south rebel boys would race around in their fast car with a confederate flag painted on it, and beat up all of the bad guys while grabbing the pretty girls. I also watched Sanford and Son, and Good Times. I appreciated both of those shows too, but the characters seemed to act as comedians, who made fun of each other, and were not as cool as the heroic characters that were shown in the White shows. These television shows along with several other brainwashing elements, made me believe that I too was White. To make things worse, I was angry with my mother for telling me that I was not.

Let's face it; media has a bigger influence in our society than we really admit to, and we must understand the purpose of who is controlling its messages before we believe in it enough to allow it teach our children.

Two

The Woman's Point Of View

Never ever allow yourself to become part of those who claim that finding the right companion is too hard or impossible. They are people who have given up and want you to become quitters like them.

By definition, a point of view is the stance by which a person's most intimate and important thoughts and ideas are brought into focus. It is how one may view or perceive any topic. To successfully comprehend the nature or the significance of a particular thing, a cogitative person must wisely select the tools that best shape and mold that individual's way of creating their points of view. Viewpoints and opinions are very important tools for expression and communication, and this chapter displays this truth from the minds of African American women.

Black women across the country are in a unique situation. They still bear the wounds from slavery, left for years to fester. Separation, mutilation, and disempowerment all left similar stinging remnants, which have also adversely affected the mindsets of both Black heterosexual men and women.

Women suffer, not only because of their baggage issues, but also because of the issues that many men bring to the table. Rather than being loved and cherished, too often do women feel that they get involved with men only to be cheated on and abused. This type of interaction becomes even less acceptable when it involves children, with whom the mothers are more frequently left to care for. Unfortunately, the understood result has created more feelings of disgruntlement toward Black men, from these women, and many times from the children as well.

The point of bringing all of this up is to reiterate the status quo. We all know about these problems. They are evident within our communities, and are not going away by osmosis. We can no longer ignore these issues that quietly and subconsciously add to our separation and isolation.

I am sure that this chapter may draw scrutiny, due to the sensitivity of its content, and I encourage such scrutiny, while suggesting that you ask yourself specific questions about what you will do to help change things. I would like for you to introspect and say, "What am I going to do to encourage positive action toward the current situation among Black men and women?" Are you going to be part of the problem or become part of the cure? If you are willing, you can change things. We all can do it together.

The Problems With Men

The current state of interaction between African American men and women is nothing less than unbalanced. The resulting frustration, created by the rifts that have separated many ties of positive communication between us has reached an all time high. These days, trusting men has become a very difficult task for many women. Granted, in many cases, men have dug the holes they stand in and have kept the shovels too.

These issues, beside others, have driven the minds of many Black men away from their families have been studied and talked about for a very long time, but when will things change? I say now, but I am just one man. Who will follow me? Better yet, who will lead with me?

Cheating, physical abuse, abandonment, imprisonment, incompatibility, lying, indolence, and addiction are just a few of the ways in which vast amounts of Black men endanger and disrespect not just their women, but their entire heritage. This has become a huge problem with our men. There are several hypothetical ideas out there dealing with reasons why many Black men act the way they do toward their women. Some say the lack of exemplary fathers in African American households contributes the most to the downgrading of women, by men. My response suggests that the lack of appreciation and consideration, across the board, is the most realistic answer.

The bottom line is that having respect for women would keep these situations from occurring at such great magnitudes. Because the effects of the lack of respect from men to women has become so obvious, I have begun to see how and why women have had such a hard time believing the truth I carry with me. Not to imply that women add to deceit by carrying out heinous acts toward men, but for the sake of this argument, we are going to only focus on men right now.

You see, even though I personally have had very little to do with the downfall of good relationship between Black men and women, it has become my responsibility to try to help my brothers see the destruction they deliver to other men, women, and children. Trust me, this frustrates me too ladies. After all, I am the one who has to hear the complaints about how I don't exist, and how I am so hard to find. So it is just as much of a burden to me, because I am my brother's keeper and sometimes that involves cleaning up his mess.

Is the Glass Half Empty Or Half Full?

How it Relates to You

During my dating experiences, I have encountered two types of women. Each type had a singular way of relating her point of view. The first type refers to women who see things from both positive and realistic positions, namely, rational women. The other type references women who bear more pessimistic mindsets. I like to call them the irrational type. While you explore this book, I hope you will be able to compare, contrast, and match the characteristics of each sort. Don't get me wrong. I do know that we all possess both rational and irrational qualities, but for the sake of explanation and introspection, let us separate the two by means of classifying personality consistencies.

First, the rational woman possesses a great sense of reality, which helps her through most situations life throws her way. She is the woman who searches for ways to better herself before suggesting that anyone else change their ways. She knows who she is, loves herself, and is guided by truth and honesty. The rational woman realizes that life presents a plentiful share of good times and bad, and she takes her realistic optimism with her wherever she goes.

Realistic optimism is a way of thinking that combines realistic thought with positive thought. Realistic optimists look at the brighter side of things, while acknowledging realistic possibilities. This type of thinking keeps the rational woman knowledgeable about the fact that she is a winner, while understanding the entire time that if she had never lost, she may have never known what winning truly was. A woman of this caliber knows that good men are everywhere, and also knows that if it is her time to be with a good man, she will seize the opportunity. All notions of male bashing, general stereotyping, and badmouthing the men of her race are nonexistent. She realizes that taking part in those actions is irrational, and such a thing would do more harm than good. Instead, she takes the time to make wise decisions about the men she chooses to date and does not settle for what she does not want. This saves her a tremendous amount of time and emotion.

The irrational woman, on the other hand, is a piece of work. She does not necessarily have the same levels of discipline or commitment as the rational woman. This type of woman has very little patience with men, usually because she tries to identify and relate the actions of one man to another. She also is not good at being able to recover from past, failed relationships quickly, so she often feels bitter and resentful. The irrational woman usually retains anger for long periods of time and thinks of why something would not work before considering how it could. In her eyes, the glass is always half-empty. Instead of taking the realistic approach by admitting that she has been with good men, with whom the relationship ended, she moves on and tells herself that she has met no good men. That definitely is not a realistic approach.

When we look at theses two types of women, the differences are obvious, but the similarities are astonishingly interesting to study. Just like the rational woman, the irrational woman has been hurt before, but her views are entirely different, partially because of the effects from painful breakups. This type of thinker usually tends to attract the wrong men and accept relationships that are no good for her. This happens for several reasons and some of these reasons revolve around complacency, pessimism, and fear of being alone. Many women who may want to flee from their failed relationships may not, due to issues of complacency and settlement. These feelings create senses of contentment and self-satisfaction, especially when coupled by the lack of awareness of danger, and controversy. Here, women happen to fall and not succeed. Many abusive relationships contain women who are complacent and afraid to leave, because they know no other way than to put up with abuse. This form of acceptance is dangerous, especially in those who deny they are in it.

The pessimistic thought, "There is nothing better out there," also ties into the complacency issue. Many harbor feelings like this and carry emotions of depression and hopelessness. They usually feel that all is lost, so they, in turn, take whatever they can get and don't set higher standards for themselves. This is a disastrous way of thinking, due to the fact that faith is a big part of success, and without it, failure is inevitable.

The rational woman holds a contrary view, while thinking, "There are good men everywhere." She just has to find the right one for her. For this woman, there is no need to settle. She remains encouraged and determined, while her faith in good brothers never diminishes.

For the irrational woman, thinking like this would lessen the destruction that she unintentionally places on herself. Her fear of being alone also adds considerably to her destructive mindset. In cases like this, single, irrational women are likely to answer and accept all callers. They usually take average offers from men and rush into situations they really aren't prepared for. With these levels of impatience and settlement, this problem leads this type of woman to abandon ideas of true love, while accepting the next best thing. This way of thinking often drives women to marry and have children before they are ready, which has become a big problem in our society.

When it is all said and done, the woman who takes the irrational approach must realize that she does not have to accept unhealthy relationships. She has the ability to escape her negative comfort zone in addition to the ability to create a positive one. I believe that the first step toward knowing where you are is to introspect and decide if you are compromising yourself by allowing negativity to cloud your decision-making and judgment. If you are, then change should become a priority. I suggest you do it here and now.

I Bet You *Love* Can Make It Better

Overall, I would like for you to become realistically optimistic when it comes to dating and more serious relationships. Never allow yourself to side with those who claim that finding the right companion is too hard or impossible. Those are people who have given up and want you to become pessimists like them. Everyone knows that misery loves company, and for that reason it is important that you create a mindset that attracts success and not failure. Negative and discouraging thoughts always lead to failure, but positive thinking always attracts success. I want you to use as many methods and strategies that you think will help improve your chances of dating or relationship success. By adopting and introducing these types of characteristics, you will definitely notice improvement in your goals.

Is There Really A Shortage Of Good Men?

I have heard from a vast number of people that there is a shortage of good, eligible African American bachelors. This has left me bewildered. I have continually been asked, "Where are all of the good men?" and I would like to answer that question, but before I do, let me define the word 'good' as I know it.

Good is a relative term that can be used in many ways. What one person may consider good, another person may consider bad. The dictionary definition of good is as follows: *Good: Being positive or desirable in nature and having the qualities that are distinguished in a particular thing; not bad or poor.* With that understanding, I want to ask a few questions of you about the good people whom you may or may not know. Please be honest.

- How many best friends have you had in your life?
- How many do you have now?
- Who are your heroes?
- How many people in this world would you do anything for, knowing that you would get the same in return?

If your answers gave you one or more individuals, then you have truly been blessed and you should be grateful for that blessing. Those would be good people. If you came up with no answers do not fear. Help is on the way. We will get you redirected by focusing on your happiness and everything else will fall into place. Trust me.

Is there a shortage? Not a chance. That is what a negative uninformed mind would have you believe. Because misery loves company, those same people gladly enjoy taking others down with them. There has never been an over-abundance of good men that up and vanished one day. There have, however, always been fewer good people than bad in the world. The numbers, in comparison, have never even been close, and this may actually be what people mean when they project their emotions verbally without taking time to think. Everyone knows that it is a lot harder to live with good characteristics and morals, than to live with negativity, laziness, and complacency.

One of my favorite guidelines states, "The path to hell is wide and broad, while the road to heaven remains straight and narrow." From this, I believe that good people, whom you can count on, are tremendously difficult to come by. This is nothing new to everyday people. With that in mind, when has it ever been easy to find good people? It has never been easy for me. This is no different from the idea of finding a good man or woman. It is actually harder because you are filtering an already rare occurrence. On top of that, finding a good Black man is yet another step in the right direction, without as abundant of a result. No matter how large the male to female ratio becomes, it will still be difficult to find good women and men. It has never been easy finding good people and still is not. We just cannot control something like that.

It is imperative that you hear the truth and remember it. Do not let your impatience for a relationship lead you to unclear thoughts that stray from reality. Also, do not allow your assumptions or emotions to force you into discouragement. Exercise strength, wisdom, and patience, and know that God's will be done for you and everyone.

What About the Shortage Of Professional Men?

Due to the amount of energy placed into the alleged 'shortage of good men' issue, I sympathize with most women who feel like they are taking a loss when it comes to the level of compatibility with professional men. However, I also wonder about the fairness in judgment of numbers referencing good, professional men.

I think one reason why some sisters don't see as many good professional men as they like is mainly because it is very difficult for good, professional men to maintain positive exterior images in this society that regularly creates new, inventive ways to strip them from their well deserved titles. Furthermore, as African Americans, our reality has become such that we do not hear as much as we should about successful, professional men without referring to rappers, athletes, and actors. Things are this way, for several reasons that do not add to our success. The main reason references how our heavy reliance on mainstream media makes it difficult for us to hold optimistic thoughts about the population of our African American, professional men. You and I both know that media does everything but support positive Blackness. What it actually does is affect our senses of reality, and it demonstrates how we do not see or hear about the masses of positive males in our American society on a whole, and how we never really have, for that matter.

Destructive presentations of America's generalized mass media population cloud our judgment daily, and because we have become so reliant on mainstream media to provide us with information, our minds have become weakened, to a great degree. Too many people are so quick to believe anything the media presents without thinking about who controls that presentation. In cases like these, I can see why many would believe how the professional Black man, on the Up High would seem like a figment of the imagination.

Lets look at Tarzan, for example. This was a show, aired back in the black and white television era that told the story of a white man in the jungles of Africa who fought the natives relentlessly with his faithful chimpanzee, *Cheetah* by his side. The native Africans were always displayed as cannibals fighting Tarzan, who was known for his famous three syllable word that we all love to hate, "Ungawa." Now, I have never been to Africa, but for such a long time I feared going because I thought I would be eaten by these Zombie-like people who wanted to catch me and my White hero. This was my only perception of my deep ancestry. Get my point? Good, lets move on.

Hearing the abundant claims from women about the lack of choice when it comes to the selection of successful, professional men concerns me. I believe that the messages, which they did not create, carry more exaggeration than truth. I partially disagree and respond by saying that Black men have made significant strides upward and continue to do so. I, personally, have seen just as many, if not more men, as I have women in all of my professional environments and am equally proud of both genders, but still explain why we need more men to place themselves in more visible positions within corporate America, so we can identify and promote amongst ourselves.

My opportunities have given me the chance to see many professional men in high managerial positions, who have inspired me immensely. I have also seen plenty of my old historically Black College friends walking through some of the most secret defense facilities in this country. My last six supervisors consisted of a group of four young African American men and two African American women who all held titles such as: Branch Chief, Director, and Group Manager. How is it that I see things differently than some women? Maybe the opinions of disbelievers are biased because of their own particular work environments. Who knows?

Sometimes, I attend after-work functions in the Washington, DC area and see more professionally dressed Black men than women. Therefore, I wonder in turn, "What is it that professional women are specifically looking for and what type of professional environments don't they think men are a part of?" I am also assuming that these same women who complain about the alleged shortage of these men, seek a high level of financial stability in their relationships. They want a man who can bring something to the table. This is an acceptable way of thinking, without being gluttonous, but I also believe that one of the big problems of today is that women with low or no income are going after upper income earners for the wrong reasons, while expecting unrealistic outcomes. Many of those types of women have had children out of wedlock and want some type of compensation to make life easier for themselves rather than for their children. They feel that they need a man to come in and save them from their despair. However, that is not an even trade to the Up High man who wants a woman with comparable willingness and consideration. Those other women usually aren't focused on marrying for love, through God. Their attention lies primarily on money and material objects. Their ideas of knowing how to treat good men come mainly through physical appearance and actions; they have no idea that real men require more.

The Up High man knows that situations like these will bring him nothing but heartache and pain. In contrast, he knows his ideal woman is out there somewhere. His problem is that lots of women believe he is extinct, and many men believe women desire them for reasons outside of love. This idea also adds insight to the topic about why women think men are afraid to commit.

My understanding is that many men value commitment, in and outside of marriage. They just want to make sure they would be doing it for the right reasons, without money or sex being the driving force. On the other hand, we have men who do not want to get married and are honest about it. These may still be good men, however, their desires are just different. The fact that a man values casual relationship does not make him unworthy, but it does make him incompatible with women who value more than just that.

Now lets get back to the so called 'shortage of men' issue, which you'll read more about in the chapter entitled *How To Find and Keep a Good Black Man*. I believe that most of the women who state this claim have probably been wronged by a man at some point and have never had much experience with a good man. Think about it for a minute. I ask myself this question all the time: "What makes women feel as though there is a shortage of men?" Then I begin to think that they actually mean to say, "I am having trouble finding the right man for me." Maybe they don't know what to look for in good men and if that is the case, how could they recognize them? I would think that a person not being able to recognize something would equally not know where to locate it, and would have significant trouble confirming its actual existence. I could see then, how one in that situation could claim, "Shortage." I usually go on to wonder if those women are being realistic and fair in their search. Are you fair in your judgment of Black men?

What's Color Got To Do With It?

Above many widespread senses of distrust and betrayal, many Black women feel as though Black men are not loyal. In entirely too many circumstances, this scenario is true, but we could all tune up our levels of devotion.

Interracial relationships often cause women to form ideas of disloyalty in their minds as well. Such thoughts cause major damage to Black men and women in relationships because their views are usually split. Overall, the Black woman feels as though she has been betrayed when she sees Black men with women of other races. Black women are even more infuriated if the couple consists of a White woman and Black man. These feelings are not always unfounded. Some women simply see it as an issue of that man ignoring the history of Black men being massacred by the hands of White men, and they also feel that the White women should just stick to their own race. Another big allegation against Black men in interracial relationships is that they abandon Black women when they reach success in order to relate to their white colleagues. My response is that this does happen, though not exactly to the degree some women claim.

Black men involved in interracial relationships are constantly reminded of the lack of growth this country has made as they are judged and labeled by insecure people. One's family members and friends may have an easier time dealing with that person's interracial relationship status, but our society has not healed from racism and prejudice enough to be able to accept the American principle, "Liberty and justice for all." Hateful stares and disrespectful comments are common responses, often directed toward both sides of interracial relationships but to the Black men who value love more than color, this type of treatment is unfair and senseless.

From a different stance, many African American men feel that they are not accepted and are ignored daily by Black women. In their eyes, the only time they notice interest from Black women is when they are with women of another race. In turn, their reaction is something like, "Oh, now you see me?" In these cases, Black men feel as though Black women act completely hypocritical, and they return the hateful looks and feelings. This causes them to make irrational statements like, "Black women have issues," or, "Black women are too angry and bitter." This type of generalizing is not fair and is counter-productive, but it does happen. I do, however, partially agree with the idea that Black men dating White women are, to an extent, betraying their own race. Some Black men are, indeed, traitors to the Black race. Those people carry the Uncle Tom label that you will read more about in Chapter three. Unfortunately, I don't have much more to say about this issue other than, Judgment day is coming and they will be served.

Naturally, Black women want to love Black men unconditionally. This is why there is so much emotion, deep-rooted within the interracial issue. The big problem is that the assortment of those emotions often remains unguided and brings about negative responses. In order for any type of mutual understanding to occur, both genders must be receptive to how each side views things. The men, who are victims of these negative results, react in many different ways. Some may flee, many fight back, some allow the mundane treatment they receive, and some overcome it by remaining patient and steadfast throughout their search for the right woman. The effects of these actions open up doors to women of other races for Black men who didn't necessarily have those doors nailed shut before. Personally speaking, my main goal in life is to be happy with or without a female companion. Therefore, I applaud any man who naturally finds happiness with a woman of any race. That is a blessing, however, I will never advocate quitting, accepting abuse, or settling for what you know will not work. If you realistically know that it is time to leave a relationship, then leave; but if you decide to switch races because you had a few bad experiences with the women or men of your own particular race, then you are a quitter and a coward. That is unacceptable, and your counterparts have a right to be angry with you.

I sympathize wholeheartedly with Black women who feel that they have exhausted all efforts to tackle successful relationships with good Black men. Some of those women have given up because they believe there is no hope. I completely understand that feeling, but those types of women do more damage to themselves by turning their backs on Black men and by treating them negatively. All this does is turn away the good men who notice the hostility from miles away. There is more provided on this issue in the chapter entitled *Interracial Relationships*.

The best examples of the origin of the Black woman's anger toward this issue stem from the fact that there have been so many cases of White's being responsible for the murdering of mass amounts of Black men. This makes many believe that a Black man would be much safer sticking to his own race. One of these shocking examples lies within the Emmett Till story. "For many, the name Emmett Till may not be familiar, but what happened to him in 1955 stunned the nation, causing shock waves that still reverberate today." The late Ed Bradley, CBS's 60 Minutes correspondent, reported that: "Till was a 14-year-old Black youngster who was murdered in Mississippi for whistling at a White woman. His death was a spark that ignited the civil rights movement in America. Two White men were put on trial for killing him, but in spite of strong evidence against them, an all-White jury acquitted them in about an hour." Fourteen-year-old Emmett Till was beaten, stabbed, shot, hung by barbed wire, and tossed into a river, where he was weighted to the bottom, all because he whistled at a White woman. Again, this is simply one incident on record that shows how bad things were for Blacks at that time, and we are still being affected by those times.

Insecurity and Intimidation

There are more and more women breaking all types of barriers and competing with men on all levels. The mindsets of the women of the world have changed, and many men have not. Some men are not aware of a proper method of response to the strength of the woman of the twenty-first century and many others react negatively. The negative reactions usually occur because of society's inability to accept the aggressiveness of contemporary women. That non-acceptance typically turns into misunderstood communication about what roles those women think men should play, based on the present level of assertiveness that many women carry. In one case, an insecure man may not wish to take a lesser role to a woman. Insecurity may cause him to feel like he is standing in her shadow or being outshone. Therefore, standing off may keep him safe in his own little chauvinistic world.

Men, if you've never had a clue before, here is your first: the most successful and aggressive women are vulnerable when it comes to their hearts. In relationships where equal backgrounds exist, most women are not ultimately focused on the idea of which partner makes the most money, as long as the man brings something to the table. If it is not money, then I suggest you be creative in finding an alternative.

No woman should ever allow herself to be held back by thoughts of relationships with men, where she feels that she must be passive about her success and assertiveness. If anything, those women should keep going and lead the way for the men who need to be taught about what is real, and correct their misconceptions.

The truth of the matter is that a strong woman may have her own home, car, and finances, but she knows that none of those takes the place of the love of a good Black man. However, many men incorrectly assume that successful women somehow replace the existence of good men with their careers, and that those women no longer need companions. This could not be any further from the truth. They are the same breed of women who value companionship and emotional fulfillment every day of their lives. They acknowledge the need for the right types of men and will not act as if they do not. However, their need does not display a message of, "I can't seem to function without you." The need is an, "I need a man to fill that spot in my life that I need him to fill," type of need. That, my friends, is a strong woman. She has the willingness to acknowledge and accept what she wants in a man, instead of acting as if she would be giving in by submitting in that manner.

Manipulation and Misrepresentation

To side with all rationalists, I can truthfully say that I would like to see more of our Black brothers and sisters attain successful, professional careers within the American work force. That would be a great thing, but we have to remind ourselves of two things.

The first reminder is that we are only a few decades out of segregation, and that we are still struggling to get past America's gigantic racial problems. Since the majority race still heads most of America's organizations and since a great amount of the majority race is *still* racist, it would seemingly be difficult to attain those professional jobs that are referred to, when discussing the lack of professional Black men.

The second reminder is that the controlled media does not focus on positive images of Blacks enough to present positive realities. Therefore, the people who are majorly reliant on television media to provide them with factual information place themselves in vulnerable positions, because of their reliance. They do this by taking on the sole responsibility of determining what is real and what is not. I cannot imagine that too many people would be able to fight off the magic behind the tube for long.

Examples of commercial media manipulation, which usually are sponsored by the unwilling and unknowing participation of Blacks, come a dime a dozen. One specific example lies within the demoralized misrepresentation of Blacks by the creation of the classic Sambo figure. Sambo was a term that was created by Whites to represent the non-competitive Negro who betrayed his own race to gain personal profit. This fictitious mockery was one of the original negative, on screen misrepresentations of Blacks through media. It was used as a comedic tool to degrade Blacks by exaggerating certain physical features and actions. Whites, at that time, used Sambo to lift their spirits and have a few laughs. Since then, Black images have gradually become more realistic on television and in the media today, but the cold reality is that media coverage still does not focus on positive male images nearly enough.

The disregarded commercial exploitation of African America is now bigger than ever. This is because those in power are able to control and manipulate the choices and opinions of others. Specific illustrations of these events display soda advertisements with a man wearing an Afro, running around using nothing but slang, while dressed in athletic wear. I don't know about you, but that sounds like Sambo to me. There are also fast food commercials that show how Calvin's entire neighborhood is so proud of his newly acquired job. They are not proud because he graduated from college or even law school. They are proud because he got a job at a cheap fast food restaurant. What's more is that there are Juice advertisements that begin by saying, "Hey momma, who drank all the Juice-AID?" I have also seen many beer commercials advertising their product by showing Black men drinking beer while being dishonest with women, just to get their attention. Personally, the first thing I thought after seeing and hearing these commercial advertisements was that those companies were using African Americans in their marketing strategies in an effort to target the interest of the Black community. Then I thought, "Why are they only portraying images of African Americans who sound ignorant and do not have enviable careers?" My answer was, "They want us to remain at a level that is lower than theirs by keeping our aspirations low, and by covering it up with a good laugh. They do this by trying to make us believe that speaking in ignorant ways brings us fame and wealth. It is plain to see how some want the world to see us and how they want us to view each other. Just ask yourself in contrast, how many television commercials you see or hear that promote convenient store, hot dog and slush drink sales, while only using people of East Indian cultures. How many other ethnicities do you see being stereotyped as African Americans are stereotyped? None! Right? I think you see my point.

The majority power's marketing strategies generally minimize African Americanism to make sure that Blacks are frowned upon, and that they benefit from it. Message!

In closing, I would like to present a plea to all Black women. Black women, you must know in your soul and mind that the Black man is not your enemy. Black man, you must know that the Black woman is not your adversary. Your enemies are the people who want to trick you into believing that the men and women of your race are inferior, hopeless, weak, and missing. We have all been misled to believe negative things about ourselves, so much that many of us have begun to hate one another and don't even realize it. This is why it is important for us to start at the root, regarding our empowerment. We have to grasp the opportunity to mend our relationships as men and women, so our children can learn the correct ways to interact with each other. We must do this, so that when they become adults they will be able to view each other equally, without disdain. We already have too many problems fighting to erase the negative racial stigma that the majority race has tried to curse upon us. Why must we continue to do this to ourselves?

By and large, there are plenty of people who have spent their entire lives searching for their ideal mates. Let us not pretend that the good Black man is on the verge of extinction by presenting fictitious statistics and irrational arguments out of anger and fear. We, together, must guide our women in the right direction so they will not outcast our Black men, because of the way another man may have treated them in the past. Also, let us not accept whatever the rumors may be about our Black brothers. Let us recognize the good Black man for who he is and for who he may want to become. Let us celebrate the good Black man, so others may see his spirit and rush to follow his lead. Let us cherish the good Black man, because he is alive and well today and wants to remain good. The truth is that the good Black man has never faded away. It is the faith in him that has. Be fair in your judgment and steadfast in your aid to heal our reconnection.

Three

The Man's Point Of View

"Believe in me I ain't like most men, I ain't like them others
You then dealt with in the past, Just have some faith
That is all I ask, believe in me."

Raheem Devaughn

Due to the great sting drawn from the effects of our haunted past, the Black man's perspective on relationships has moved far from that of the Black woman's. There are so many obstacles that have been placed in between both sides that they each have begun to think that they placed them there intentionally. As a result, some Black men are made to feel like they have to put up with unjust treatment from Black women in order to love them. In addition, the experiences of numerous Black men have revealed that it has become very difficult to find good Black women who allow them to start off with clean slates. To those good, honest men it almost seems as though they walk into debt without even making a purchase. Who wants that? Actualities like this wrongfully turn the honored American judicial system's "Innocent until proven guilty," into, "Guilty until proven innocent."

There were many instances in my past where I was made to feel like I had done something wrong when I hadn't. I have personally ended many dating situations because of the fact that those particular women felt as though they had to use methods of interrogation, in order to discover my whereabouts, along with the company I kept. They felt as though I was guilty of some bad deed, but denied that feeling each time I enquired about it. The types of methods I speak of consisted of dozens of challenging questions regarding where I was, who I was with, and if my company was of the male or female gender. The funny thing about this was that all of those intrusively probing questions would always come before even asking me if I had a good time doing whatever I had been doing. Their probing made me feel like a criminal, and we all know that no honest person working hard at their relationship wants to feel like they have committed a crime when they haven't. "Why does she feel that she has to ask me questions in this manner?" I thought to myself. "Doesn't she know that she can ask, using a kind approach with a calm voice?" These questions raced through my mind, because I felt insulted that the women in those situations felt like they had to ask me questions with intrusive strategies. It seemed as if they felt they had to challenge my honesty each time I stepped outside of the house, and that was not fair to me.

The Monster Bash

Being an overly forthcoming person, I am forced to reiterate that problems with male bashing, along with other malicious general stereotypical attacks toward the Black male gender, are processes acted out by narrow minded individuals who don't take the time to think about the effects of their unfair actions. Overall, it has also been unpleasant to witness women stomping down unforgiving paths to bash all men, while remaining in relationships with the same old obvious players time after time. Aside from that, male bashing along with other general stereotypes related to the male gender are biased acts of prejudice. If anybody knows how wrong this type of group discrimination is, it is Black people. We should all be aware that any attempt at implying that the intent and action of an entire group is uniform, because of the actions of a few of the members, is unjust.

There was once a time when open stereotypes were placed on Blacks regarding their alleged lack of intelligence, ability, and many other things. According to the popular belief of that time, Blacks were supposedly incapable of flying airplanes, running businesses, and even holding the football position of quarterback. Those misconceptions presently sound silly don't they? In the past, acts like these have only added to our separation, but it does not have to be like that now.

On another note, as humans, we are social beings and need companionship to survive. There are ways to work around the issue of not having a mate, but one would need a great amount of patience to practice those ways. I believe that women who don't think they can be happy without men will do anything to prevent loneliness. Sometimes a woman may not wait for what she really wants and needs. Instead, she will settle for what is presented to her. It almost makes it seem as though she never learned from the mistakes she made previously, given that she continues to choose the same types of men from past, disastrous relationships. In situations similar to these, it appears as though women sometimes date the wrong men, while maintaining the hope that they will change them some how. These women should know that people don't change just because someone wants them to. If the types of men a woman dates don't seem to be working out at all, why would that woman keep dipping her hand back into the same bucket of men with the same characteristics?

Too many women get stuck repeating the same mistakes in their relationships. Most times, this keeps them from finding the happiness they think they deserve. Why not pick from the other side of the road where the fruit is more ripe? That is, if those women are able to recognize bad fruit when they see it in. However, they should also be able to recognize good fruit. The bottom line is that the good Black man is everywhere and is waiting to be noticed, appreciated, and picked from the tree of Up Highness.

I know that there are situations with women when the bad guys slip through the radars undetected, but even that would be less likely to happen if women practiced the simple steps of preparation that are provided within the *How to Find and Keep a Good Black Man* chapter. You will see there, that self-preparation, as a foundation, should be used as the key in fundamentally productive dating practices.

A Better Approach

My experiences as a youth showed me that there were lots of Black women who were generally angry with Black men without knowing why. It sounds odd, but it is a reality for many. Most of those women had been made to suffer so bad that their methods were changed across the board.

As a young man, I was hurt several times by women. The wise choices I made as a result of learning from my misfortunes benefited me by allowing me to make the decision to become strategically focused on the types of individuals I allowed into my personal space. I began to believe that fairness should always be embraced at the beginning of relationships and should remain throughout. I knew that using this approach would greatly improve the consistency of my interactions with people of good quality and values.

The plan was difficult to implement but effortless for me to sustain. First, I sat down and asked myself a few questions. I said, "Self, what do I want and what don't I want in both a dating and committed relationship? Do I know the difference between the two, and have I decided which is better for me at this time?" After I answered those questions along with a few others, I found several ways to separate women based on the characteristics and qualities they presented. I then began to notice behavioral patterns with certain types of women, which made the acceptance and elimination processes of dating much easier for me. This way, I felt no need to change, judge, or label anyone. I simply eliminated the women with qualities I was not interested in, and accepted the women with more of the qualities I was interested in.

To all women who have been hurt, I believe that you have a right to be angry with the particular person who hurt you, but you also have the right to remain intelligent, determined, encouraged, and strong. Dating, and the process of what was traditionally called courtship are unarguably risky gambles. When it comes to selection, however, you will be happier if you do not settle for just any pretty package. Be strong and wait for the real thing. If you want better chances with dating and commitment, the wise choice is to figure out what you want to achieve from dating, without settling for anything less.

It is not right for women to group Black men by using *all* men as their reference point. Because their experiences and, or the experiences of others have threatened their trust in men, their emotions guide them to believe the only answer has to be that all men are screwing up somehow. I do sympathize with women who feel the need to interact in these ways, but I also disagree with the way they are going about opposing their problems. I believe the feelings of those women are authentic, but their reasoning is a bit misguided. To protect themselves from being hurt, those women train their minds to view men as untrustworthy, dangerous investments, and because they have been treated badly so much, both personally and remotely, they now succumb to the pain by male bashing and cutting men off all together. When this happens, it forces these women to act as though good men are on the brink of extinction by seeking answers and coming up with unrealistic hypotheses regarding their own personal situations.

I believe that the best way for women to fight the habitual acts of subconsciously downing all men is to be real with themselves and honor fairness. They should realize how wrong they are when they group all men together, because not only does it cause other women to take steps backwards, it also makes the men who work hard at being good and desire to be good husbands and companions think twice about doing such righteous things. What this process also does is cut off all chances for any type of brother to have a fair shot at gaining women's trust. In turn, this forces those men to view women in hypocritical ways, thus creating negative trust issues on both sides. Men who face these problems sometimes feel as though they do tremendous amounts of work in their efforts to be good and wholesome men for themselves and their women, only to be slapped in the face when they hear those references about all men being a certain way. What this does to a man who strives to be good to the woman he chooses, is make him feel as though his work is invalid. When that happens it discourages him from wanting to be as good of a man, as he gets the same result either way.

Worthlessness is the lowest blow one could hand to a man who is really trying, and we, as men and women, are dealing that blow to ourselves. It is imperative that we use the necessary tools to spark needed change immediately.

Here I Am, Can't You See Me?

Ariel was around eight years old when she started asking her mom about boys. Her mother was a single parent at the time and received parental assistance from her mother and older sister. The little girl went to school every day and was very bright. She was so mature that she only hung out with the ten and eleven year old girls at school.

Ariel would see her mother and aunt going in and out of relationships while crying a lot about their lack of success. She hated watching her mom yell and scream at her boyfriends and began to collect a great disdain for the men. Day after day, she went to school and told her girlfriends what she had been witnessing, only to find out that some of them had been going through similar situations and hated their mother's boyfriends as well.

Over time and many conversations later, Ariel, at 15, thought she had a full understanding of what boys wanted. She listened to her mom, grandmother, aunt, and girlfriends preach so much, that the warnings against men had become more than true. She heard all of the negative complaints and cautions similar to, "Men ain't shit, there are no good men around, and all they want is your sex," in addition to the best one of all, "All good Black men are dead, gay, or in jail." So needless to say, by this point, Ariel had such a negatively militant outlook on her future with men that she was blinded by disgust.

Eleven years pass by, and Mr. London Jones walks along the sidewalk in his business suit, after leaving an afternoon meeting with his colleagues. London is a successful twenty seven year old, single gentleman in the technical industry, who is taking life by the horns. He stands about six and a half feet tall with an athletic build and a stunning smile. Young Mr. Jones pleasantly walks along, while approaching this gorgeous young woman with an obvious appearance of distinguished class. As she draws near, London silently loses his mind as a result of this woman's beauty. From ten feet away, London sees the woman's name tag and quickly greets her with a smile and says, "Hello, Ariel. How are you doing on this beautiful day?" All of a sudden, London frowns in confusion, as the woman angrily scowls at him, sucks her teeth, and keeps on walking. The disappointed man stands in amazement and blames himself for even speaking at all, while thinking, "What is it they don't see in me? Do they see me at all? I feel like something may be wrong with me," he thought to himself.

The interesting point here is that the future decisions London will make, based on his emotions, will ultimately determine what kind of man he will want to become and what types of relationships he would want to be involved in, if any at all.

The message from this story is simple. There are many women who teach their daughters, granddaughters, and nieces to defend themselves against the bad men who want to come and steal their innocence. I agree and equally encourage this type of instruction. However, the problem lies in the fact that this lesson is the main source of attention for many Black single women, and it formulates into negative energy most times.

Ladies, as teachers, you cannot just talk about bad men and be completely successful with covering all ends of the spectrum. Not only do our young ones need to protect themselves from the bad men and women of the world, they also need to protect themselves from falling into the same stereotypical pitfalls that many of us have plummeted into ourselves. This alone would uncover the veil, which has been placed over the good man's head and image. Children, and adults alike should all know about the good Black man on the big screen, over the radio, and in books. If you leave him out of your teachings, then he may not exist at all in their minds.

Ariel passed up a chance with a good man because she had been scarred so much that she had begun to allow her images of some men to mix in the same pot as the rest, which left her with no idea of how to recognize an honest, good man. She knew that many men were known to perpetuate kindness for their own deceitful reasons, but what she was not aware of was that those men were actually imitating the good man, whose statements always held truth and sincerity. Although she thought she was ready, she was not prepared for the arrival of her desires. She only knew what she didn't want, as opposed to knowing both what she did and did not want. This made it impossible for her to recognize her goal.

What Do Women Really Want?

We all know that women are the most emotional creatures on the face of the planet. This is no secret and is the reason why men are so fascinated with the female gender, but the truth about those emotions is never predictable. On one hand, a man could find himself in a realm of euphoria, delivered by the hand of a woman. On the other hand, devastation served at its coldest temperature could appear out of nowhere or come swiftly, after betraying her trust. Though my statements may seem rhetorical, my points only symbolize the almost certain and unclear acts of judgment women make in reference to men.

Women who can't find the specific type of men they want to be with, sometimes search for reasons why they fail and blurt out the first thoughts that come to mind. This can be dangerous, because when dealing with uncontrolled emotion, any answer could attract their desire to know. Such fast paced judgment that often follows, tends to lead to incorrect assumptions and wrongful accusations. The blame in these situations usually gets passed around and directed away from where it should end up.

When it comes to men and the lack there of, many women's 'missing in action' label often gets handed out like pancakes at a lumberjack convention. Their claims of not enough men doing this or that always rise to the top of their lists of why they are not getting what they want. My questions to the women who make those claims are, "Is it really men who are the problem?" "Could your selection in men use a little revising?" "Do you think you would bring as much to the table as you would want your ideal man to?"

My problem with some women is also that they subliminally look for handouts while getting to know men. They think that just because they have a vagina, every man should fall down and beg for their attention. They'll sing that song, "Can you pay my bills," but won't even have a clue about what it takes to treat a worthy man like a good man should be treated. Maybe the weak, frail minded men fall for that, but strong, intelligent men know better. The truth is that there are many men who have problems with women who do nothing but complain and nag, while sitting on their butts, not doing anything with their lives, and still expecting men to submit to their every desire. The funny thing is that when it doesn't happen, they cry about there not being any potential candidates around. Then, all of a sudden, you have an issue of a nation-wide shortage of African American males within the population. Am I right or wrong?

To the women who do nothing but complain, whether you have good men or not, "You must find a better way." The more time you spend complaining about your situation, the less time you are using to do something about it. Good Black men suffer because of you and your words. Don't they already have it hard enough? Please stop being hindrances, and support the cause. Use your strength to force men to treat you with more respect and honor. Better yet, by killing your negativity alone, you will force good men to notice and accept you more, instead of driving them away.

The end all is this; if a woman wants a better man, she may have to become a better woman. Remember, he wants a keeper as well. Some may deserve the abuse, but please stop giving your hard-working men bad names.

Stop Making Everything a Man Issue

The blame game is something else, isn't it? It has come to my attention that the ratio of women to men has become a huge focal point for thousands of women who claim, "Men have it so much easier than women do." That being a general exaggeration, of course. Those women also say that this topic presents the main reason why men are so dishonest and promiscuous. Even though the second reason may hold more truth than the first, this truth does not fall in the laps of all men. Now, the ratio I refer to is a quotient that has always displayed imbalance. Women have always outnumbered men and yes, men have always cheated. However, I must reiterate by saying, "That number does not include all men."

To go further with this mathematical example, let's do a little realistic number crunching. What women and men alike say about the horrific amount of unavailable men is true to some degree. Jails accross America have become overpopulated with African American convicts, and America's Black, gay population soars beyond any traditional churchgoer's comprehension. Between the extremely large amount of absent fathers, liars, cheaters, and betrayers, the situation for our men is looking very grim.

We already know that these issues among others are hardly old news to us, but we must also understand that they are the same issues that other races deal with as well. It just happens to be that Black men are in a little deeper than they should be, because as a group, we are failing to learn our lessons, and the remedy is much more difficult to apply than it would be for other American men of different heritages.

I believe that the majority of women who are out there making strong allegations against men are guilty of a few things themselves and should be the last to cast stones. Remember, we are in this situation together ladies and gentlemen. This is not a time for tit for tat, but let's switch views for a moment. What is the deal with women who have kids with good men and don't let the fathers see their children? Do those women complain about a lack of good men? Sure they do. Are men the problem though? What about women in jail, prostitutes, and women who have baggage with walls and no windows or doors? What about lesbian women and women who choose to be by themselves? What about gold diggers, cheating women, and male bashers? The ball lies on both sides of the fence. What are your thoughts about this?

For single Black men, it can be just as difficult to find the right partner as it often is for Black women. When it comes to what people bring to the table, real men want women with benefits, just as women desire from men. Everyone has their preference, but should men not date women who work in grocery stores, nail shops, or fast food restaurants because they think those *unfavorable* jobs make them bad women? Heck no. So why is it ok for women to judge men that way? Also, is every woman who complains about the alleged shortage of men doing everything she can to ensure that man's comfort and security with her? Let's keep it real. You see, in life there are aggressive people who make things happen. Then there are people who sit around and complain about what they think is happening. They never know what is really going on because they are always too busy being safe and comfortable. That, my friends, is no man or woman issue. That is what I call human imperfection.

What many women need to do is stop blaming men and focus on the bigger picture. Should Black men be more honest about their feelings toward Black women? Of course they should, but that hardly implies that all or even most men are dishonest individuals. Women and men both need to be more honest with each other. Let's top making it a man issue.

What We Need To Do Now

Some say young men and women are usually results of what their parents did or did not teach them. Since this is so, let us strive to do a better job in teaching our children to make intelligent decisions and remain loving at the same time. Let us encourage each other more, so we may have more faith in what we need and deserve, but not necessarily what we desire or lust for.

Go Moms and Dads! Teach your daughters about the bad men who want to steal their innocence away. Teach your sons about the bad women who want to break their pure hearts by using them for their strengths and accomplishments. Lastly, parents, please remember to include one very important thing in your teachings. Remember to educate your children about the men and women who will accept them, care for them, trust, and appreciate who they are as people. Don't just teach them how to protect themselves from others. Teach them how to grow with them.

Trust

Trust has become a very big issue among Black Americans over the years. Ever so often do we look at our brothers and sisters with a suspicious eye? We guard our very own territory and hide our secrets because of the possibility of being taken advantage of. We compete in the workplace, while feeling that there is only room for self. We selfishly do whatever it takes to make sure that we are the ones who will succeed, but remain cautious about helping the next brother or sister achieve his or her accomplishments. Too often are we competitors in love as well. We strive to demean our so-called Black rivals while assuming their every action to be a form of deception. Because of our accumulating distrust for one another, hate grows within, and if we do not learn to trust each other soon, our fate will be a very difficult one to swallow.

Our problems with trust originated hundreds of years ago when Whites would hire Black informants to spy on other Blacks within slave plantations and report back to White Slave Masters. In turn, they were given White favor. The name given to those servants was Uncle Tom. A more detailed definition of this term comes from Random House Dictionary, 1987 edition, which states: *"Uncle Tom, disparaging and offensive. A Black man considered by other Blacks to be subservient to, or to curry favor with Whites."* This snitch-like character was motivated by Whites to separate the communication of Blacks, which would inevitably create distrust among them. Other Blacks hated the Uncle Tom figure that firmly stood in the way of their freedom. Rarely were captives able to uncover the identity of the snitch, so in fear of their own privacy, they became suspicious of each other. At that point, everyone was viewed as a suspect, and the ultimate result revealed itself as a tightening of the social lines within African America. This also contributed to the increase in tension between Black males and Black females. This poisonous hatred has sadly been passed through the generations without wide acknowledgment of its cause, and still remains to be a problem.

Educating ourselves and our young ones about the historical realities of why we engage in the many negative relational environments that we do would deliver a necessary blow to the misunderstandings that we have about one another. What is your opinion?

Play On Playette

Recently, the strategies I have seen women use have intrigued me to a great degree. I have found that playing, or the act of being a player or playette, has become an action that many women have adopted and developed to some degree. This happens for many reasons, but most times, anger is the cause for their adaptation to playerism. Women feel they have put up with so much crap from men for so long that they just want to put their emotions aside and interact in other fashions. Other player-istic reasons *de la femme* involve those who try to increase the odds of finding that special someone by dating multiple men at once. Alternatively, because of the great inheritance of natural emotion that women are graced with, becoming playettes ultimately does more harm than good. Let's look into this a little by noting how women are generally more in touch with their emotions than men are. Don't get me wrong; I am not suggesting that men have fewer emotions than women do, because we all experience the same emotions, just not at the same degree. I am, however, stating that men are generally able to hold back a little better. Please don't hate me for saying it. It is what it is.

In cases where you have a one woman man who is dating three women of his preferred liking, and a woman who is dating three men with whom she is also happy, there will usually be two different outcomes. If the woman, who had an original goal of settling down with one man, finds that she has feelings for all three, "Houston we have a problem." The general truth is that women are not naturally successful with juggling their emotions. It is also true that men usually and naturally have the tendency to consume much of the woman's overall time and emotion. This situation creates a problem for the playette, who just wants one man.

One-woman men who use the strategy of dating multiple women generally have an easier time letting other women go. This is so because men are generally slower than women are with accruing long lasting feelings. The other women may be wanted, but at the same time, the man has to weigh his options and gamble intelligently. For the women who just want to dog men, this method of playerism may work, however, a woman in search of a lifelong companion would have better chances sticking with one person at a time.

Hippity Hop

I wrote about Hip Hop several times in this book because it is important to me. I love its positive core and culture. The Hip Hop art form had a very strong effect on my upbringing and I know that it affects others as well. It has a great bearing on what we do and how we act within our daily lives, as well as within our relationships. Positive Hip Hop affects an enormous amount of African America in a good way and I would never place blanket accusations or the blame of negative outcomes in our race onto its name. Nonetheless, it has become clear to me that many recent Hip Hop song and video themes have presented displays of Black men as pimps and thugs, who have reached certain levels of fame and success by way of their theatrical representations through music and videos. Most of these so-called artists brag about their prior or present experiences with drugs, murder, gangs, money, and women. These issues are obviously not righteous claims to positive things, but are attractive to many. Their messages show how their circumstances did nothing to change their personalities for the better. Talking about their realities only seemed to have fattened their pockets a little. To me, it seems like they worship money and not God. These same artists are usually eager to degrade Black women in their lyrics and video representations, by exploiting their bodies and by referring to them in profane manners!

Regarding the words of identification that we use to reference each other, Hip Hop has definitely had its impact on the mindsets of every-day, ordinary people. Simply understanding our useage of terminology has made it very clear how strong Hip Hop's influence is within our lives. A male, for instance, is sometimes called a Pimp or a Player. If he had any luck, he could even get one of his boys to call him, "My Nigga," while a sister is easily referred to as a bitch or ho (whore), when they really are neither. What is that all about? When did we get such things turned around? Fortunately, these specific realities are no fault of Hip Hop's, although it has become the vehicle that certain individuals use to direct their messages. The blame should be placed on the studio ruffians who call themselves artists, in an effort to make money by destructively abusing Hip Hop while misusing its name.

Take a deep look inside our actions of self-prejudice and see how many hip hop music videos are flooded with light skinned Black women, multiracial women, and women of other ethnicities, who flock to these rap stars who always have money in their hands and a superfluous amount of *bling* around their necks and wrists. Those women blissfully dance, while sporting their flawless bodies in stringy bikinis. What kind of effect do you think this leaves in the minds of viewers? Positive, negative, or both? To me, there's nothing wrong with seeing gorgeous women in videos. I never said I don't like watching beautiful women dance, however, the lack of beautiful, brown-textured, clothed women in music videos has made me very curious. Also, if the direction of rap songs contained more positive and meaningful messages, would women feel the need to exploit their bodies so often? Do you remember the Mary J. Blige video with the girls in the baseball caps, jerseys, and kneepads? Man, those dancers were the hottest brown honies, and they had on plenty of clothes. Wooh! I sure would like to see that video again.

Okay, getting back to the point. Mainstream rappers also rarely use anything other than fair-skinned Black and Puerto Rican women in their videos, who appear to be their rewards to fame. Those women are usually very exotic, beautiful, and tend to not be the concern. The problem is that these overly consistent images are exclusively utilized and propelled into the minds of Black men, women, and children. They force a standard of what the people controlling media view as beautiful. What this does to the minds and viewpoints of children, teenagers, and adults who don't realize the endangerment of their future is make them more comfortable with solely correlating beauty with light skinned, stringy-haired images. This, in turn, makes Black beauty seem non-existent. In retrospect, the played-out images of thugs and light-skinned, longhaired women have somewhat defined what should be accepted and favored in society. They have unfairly become the manipulated desires and poster image ideals that have replaced regular images of good, realistic Black men and women, and that is very sad.

The strength and influence of media is more powerful than most of us realize. The big problem with this incorrectly guided strength is that it makes it difficult for the individuals who rely on television for information to maintain fair views of themselves and others. Women who rely heavily on television media may not have the tools to successfully tell the difference between a thug and an Up High brother. Even if she knew the difference between the two, she more than likely would not choose the Up High man, because what she would see as favorable would be diamonds, cars, and money. Men, in turn, would shun brown skinned women for women of lighter complexions, with curly or straight hair, and treat darker skinned women like the bottom of the barrel. What good do you think this does for our trust?

I Wonder Why They Call Me Pimp

In the fifth grade, after telling my friends that I had a girlfriend, they called me names similar to Casanova and lover boy. If I were growing up today, I would probably be called pimp, but fifth graders don't know anything about pimping or prostitution right? At least they shouldn't.

Pimping is not an illustrious means of securing a profitable future, so why is it an enviable title for children? Is it really a good career move for a Black person to become a pimp or ho? Maybe you think I am over-analyzing this idea. If so, would you tell your son or daughter that you wanted him or her to become a pimp or ho, so they could have a better future? The answer is no, right? So, because the answer is no, it should be your duty to help your kids and adult associates choose other terms of appreciation and achievement for themselves. This way, we wouldn't have to place so much of the blame of our troubles on the influence of movies and videos. We would have responsible parents and leaders to look to for guidance. Any man who wants his son to become a pimp is insane in my book, and this is my book, which I wrote to uplift the Up High man, not prostitution.

The Reasons Why We Appear To Be Stuck

The strategic plans to destroy Black families, such as the manipulation of media, alongside countless others, have been used for centuries to break the spirits of Blacks. The idea has always been to turn us against our own. What better way to do that than by making us hate one another? If we hate our own Blackness, we will hate each other. If we believe that our Blackness is ugly, then it will be. It is up to us to change the way we view ourselves.

It is remarkable how something as simple as television has the capability to influence the minds of so many people. This is why there are people and corporations who battle these mockeries and fight for more positive Black media representation. What we need is a level playing field, and the people who control the playing fields do not want us to have one. This is our reality. They want us to hate the images of ourselves, so we won't produce beautiful, intelligent Black children to enlighten the world. Their desire is for Black women to choose the wrong type of men and have no hope for anything better.

You must understand that our misfortune was planned, and we suffer because of it. Our placement is not our fault but it has become our responsibility and destiny to overcome. We, now, must realize this and stop blaming each other. We must understand who has placed our pitfalls in front of us and step out of the hole that they have put us in.

Presently, we have two Black television sources and more organized radio network stations than ever before. We have definitely come a very long way. I smile every time I think about this, but I still want more for us. I really am not satisfied at all. I have the desire for Black television to display more realistic representations within productions, outside of Good

Times and Sanford and Son, as well as B and C classed movies. I am aware that those illustrations are funny, but most of the shows were filmed back in the 1970s & 1980s and do not reflect today's progress for Blacks. In the past, I sat around and watched people laugh at those shows, who have not known how to turn them off in their heads. It is now time for us to produce fresh television displays that represent who we are and who we may want to become.

In the Middle Of It All

In the seventh grade, I attended a public middle school in Hyattsville, Maryland, where the enrollment contained a predominant number of mixed ethnicities. During this time, my goal was to fit in with other kids, but it was hard for me to do that when my mother was struggling with the bills and taking care of my sick grandfather, in addition to me. Having little money made it very difficult for us. My entire wardrobe consisted of about two pairs of sweatpants, one pair of jeans, a few raggedy T-shirts, and a couple of (s)medium sized sweatshirts, if you catch my drift. I'm sure you can understand from this that I was forced to recycle clothing sets several times a week. The other kids noticed my situation instantly and were not quiet about it. I was even ridiculed by the poor ones who wanted to uplift themselves by pointing out my misfortune. The Black girls usually led the group attacks on my person, but I couldn't understand why they wanted to hurt me so bad and so often. "What did I do to deserve this?" I thought. I began to hate myself and dislike my mother for placing me in that situation. Daily, relentless attacks left me scarred and clueless, but I moved on.

Because I knew I had no chance with the Black girls at school, I responded to an interest that was offered to me by a nice looking Italian girl. I immediately became excited when I realized that a girl actually liked me. She was very nice, and helped me feel good about myself during that time, even though she knew about my issues. She didn't judge me, but liked me for who I was. Once the Black girls caught wind of what was going on, they called me all sorts of treacherous names, implying that I betrayed them. I was referred to as, "White girl lover" among other things. At that point, I was furious. "How dare they insult me when they exiled me," I thought. Anger and confusion led me to respond with allegations of hypocrisy toward the Black girls. "We never wanted you in the first place," they shouted. "I know, so why are you acting like you care now?"

I hollered back. This reminded me of the saying, "Don't argue with fools because people who are watching can't tell who is who." You see, what I didn't know at that time was that there was so much pain and frustration in the hearts of those females that they had little to no control over their emotions. It was foolish for them to judge me, and it was equally foolish for me to add more pain to their hearts by responding negatively. The Up High man would have tried to console and comfort those sisters while reaffirming the encouraging reality that things will get better.

Relating to these experiences in addition to many others, makes me believe that Black women need to feel more love from good Black men and Black men need to feel more appreciation and support from good Black women. We all know that there are bad people everywhere, but that badness does not affect everyone. We must believe these realities before our issues of trust can be healed. Good Black men should not be forced to feel like they are diseased when approaching Black women. Good Black women should not be stereotyped as groups of angry male bashers. We need to put our emotions aside, so we can get a better grasp on reality. The faster we accept and understand our reality, the faster we will come together as Black men and women. Let's get it done. The time is now.

Four

The Successful Black Man

"Let us not become weary in doing good, for at the proper time, we will reap a harvest if we do not give up."
Galatians 6:9

When referring to the mission of finding good, successful Black men, the first thing we should realize is that the terms 'good' and 'successful' can be split. What one person considers good, another person may consider bad and vice versa. Fancy cars and luxurious homes, on the other hand, may define success, for some. Others may see success in a totally different light.

What is success? Success is the achievement of a sought after goal. A good, successful Black man is a man who accomplishes, or who is motivated to accomplish the goals he has desired, planned, or attempted to achieve. Even though there are several types of successful men, these men all have one thing in common. They are all men who work to get where they want to be in life and have all grasped some measure of success in one way or another. Though reaching their goals of success is always a virtuous feat, others don't always share that type of awareness.

In reference to dating, some look at successful men and say they should not have any problems finding good, wholesome women, but assumptions like those are far from accurate. Some may also suggest that the abundance of Black women in America creates such a wide ratio that finding a suitable mate, for a successful Black man, should be an automatic and simple task. Once again, this is not true. There is one obvious reality pertaining to this situation that sheds light on this matter, and that is that there are many more Black women in America than there are Black men. This, however, does not mean that every Black man has dozens of perfect women to choose from at his leisure. Let's keep it real. In no way is it easier for men to find suitable mates than it is for women. No matter what the latest ratio happens to be, the reality for many successful, good African American men is that it is just as difficult to find compatible partners of the opposite sex with similar values within the parameters of communication, consideration, spirituality *etc.*

In *The Most Popular 12 Myths* chapter, I display several details dealing with the myth of there being a shortage of good, successful Black men in the professional world. In that section, the message also emphasizes the importance of understanding how devastating it can be to compare professional White men in their occupations to professional Black men in theirs. It further implies that fighting for deserved jobs should always be the goal, but suggests that no one should ever define a Black man by comparing him to White men who have been passing down their Black made wealth for generations. The facts that American White men have a combined wealth greater than all Black men, and have built their foundations from the labor of Blacks, is a result of what I like to call the 'good old boy' network. It is a simple concept of, "It's my ball and you can't play." Black men have, in retrospect, raised the bar by accepting the challenge and have moved forward. This does not mean that there is now a level playing field, but it does imply that success-seeking Black men are doing a hell of a job to make it a level playing field.

Ironically, there have also been too many instances where the 'good' label has been left off of the Black man's title, because he didn't have that stellar job, financial stability, or flawless home, in the eyes of others. Do these things really define a person's worth? Why can't the sisters complaining about this so-called 'shortage' of Black professional men see the entire picture? Is it possible for good, professional men to work without wearing suits, while making less than $50,000 to $100,000 a year, and not lose his glorious title? Also, why can't teachers, security guards, and bus drivers share in the glory? What makes them such undesirably unprofessional men, and why is that so? Must I work as a doctor, lawyer, athlete, or rapper to catch the finest Black woman out there? It seems like it, for a lot of good brothers.

Ladies, I know you all want that gorgeous man within your age range, who will take care of you, and who has a college education, with no kids, and a heightened career status, but you have to ask yourself, "How likely am I to find any man with all those qualifications, who is willing to accept the issues that I may bringing to the table?" I'm just going to let that one marinate and suggest that we really look inside of ourselves and ask, "Am I being fair to myself and to others?" Also, "Am I, at times, hypocritical in my search for companionship?" Lastly, "Does what I want match up with the way I am going about acquiring it?"

My advice is this: everyone should know that good, successful Black men look for the same beneficial characteristics in women as well. Do you agree or disagree?

In this next case I use the label '*good women*' to refer to women who are compatible with, and who are good for Up High men.

Ron Wills once wrote in an article, "A successful Black man, in most cases, will not grab any woman he sees." Men want to date someone on their level as well. A successful brother is going to want a certain level of classification, education, and enlightenment in a mate. He is typically not going to want a woman whose biggest desire is to have her hair and nails done every day.

The truth is that there are several things a good man considers when he searches for a good woman, but the biggest concern is compatibility. Many women happen to make the mistake of placing commitment before compatibility, but a good, successful Black man knows that not to be the correct order of operation for a successful relationship.

The future is also important to the good, successful Black man. This is so because it is equally important that he remains able to match and share equal values with his prospective mate. Female to male ratios don't really mean much to him because there are only a select few women that he would be compatible with anyway. You will see that it is all just a numbers game if you do the math. Let's use Quincy for example.

Quincy is a career successful college graduate who owns a home and drives a nice car. After meeting ten Black, professional women within the past three weeks, he reviews their qualities and realizes that out of the group, four have one or more children. Quincy likes kids, but isn't comfortable with the Baby's Daddy issue, so that kind of takes those women out of the game. Two of the remaining six have nasty smoking habits and the prettiest one out of the entire group is marked for elimination because she carries so much baggage from previous relationships that male bashing, for her, seems to be a consistently natural occurrence. Unfortunately, one woman is really nice, but because of her demanding schedule, isn't able to go out on dates as often as Quincy likes, so they are going to remain friends.

If you did your math correctly, then you already know that this leaves two women out of ten, who have made it through the process of elimination. I'm sure that Quincy hopes he hasn't wasted all of his time and is able to make a strong connection with one of them.

I trust that this example gives you some idea about how difficult it can be for good men during the stages of courtship. It is rarely a simple task to grasp total success, for men who seek it. I also hope that this example helps you become familiar with formulating your own opinions about why you think the selection process of dating is so difficult for a great number of our people including yourself, if you are currently dating. Lastly, I really want you to realize that it has been a tough road for our good men and good women together.

My examples describe only a few cases of how difficult dating can be for good Black brothers and sisters. There are a lot of lonely brothers out there who carry similar feelings that many sisters do, both negative and positive alike. There are just so many angry distractions between us most times, that we don't take time out to see things from both sides. My plea to you is that you look at both perspectives and come up with your own fair and equal interpretation and solution. We must do something now, and we can start right here with you and I. If we do not, then it is no one's fault but our own.

Five

Looking For Love In the Wrong Places

"We will always stumble in our relationships if God is not our foundation. Games, unrealistic expectations, and not knowing yourself are things that sabotage marriages and relationships. To make things worse, we dive into the physical aspects before we even know whom we are dealing with."

Wendy Parker

I spent the entirety of my teenage years baffled by some of the choices girls and women made about the boys and men they chose to be with. I felt like I was often over-looked when it came to the selection process, and I still do at times. I could not understand how or why females kept hurting themselves when the solutions to their problems seemed so simple. Because they didn't take time to observe the distinct personality characteristics of the men they chose, these women ended up in disappointing situations. As a result, they felt tricked and betrayed and labeled the men accordingly. If they had looked in the right place for the men they wanted, their chances would have been better.

As people, we are gifted with a certain motivation that allows us to create goals, however, we also have habits that force us off of the paths that lead us to our goals. The goals I speak of come with risks that make both parties vulnerable during the early stages of relationships. Like the example above, those risks can turn into disaster if one doesn't look in the right places for their potential companion's inner characteristics. The solution for this is straightforward. Stay on the right path by looking in the right places instead of all the wrong ones.

Women often make the mistake of searching for men in places that complement themselves, and that isn't always a good thing. While the attraction for material and physical items does much to draw many women in, these distinctions do not necessarily equate to the stability or longevity of a good man's worth. This has become a problem for many women who seek good men with great benefits, because they generally become excited about profiting and don't take time to view what inspires those men. Therefore, the material and physical attributes become their desire, in place of the actual man. From this, it is clear to see how people like postal workers and single fathers with sole custody of their children could have hard times finding women who would think differently of them.

Some women also say that becoming more intimate and knowledgeable about the characteristics and values of the men who pursue them does little to ensure 100% effectiveness against ending up with a bad guy. I totally agree with them and believe that there is not one foolproof method for fending off the wolves, but the likelihood of raising the successes rate of better selection in men would increase instantly by leading a proactive effort. Not only would women benefit from it, but men would also get their acts together to obtain the favor of the women they pursue. This would inspire lazy men who feel as though they have it made, to go through their own processes of introspection and step their games up. Some people call it shaping up or shipping out. What women need to do is light a fire up underneath their hind-parts and let those men know that they are not going to take it anymore. Women, you have more potential than you give yourselves credit for, and you can choose your destiny by being more wise and patient in your choices. What sisters have to do is grasp the power they hold over men and use it proactively.

Women may not always have control over their emotions but they are naturally stronger than men in the mental department. Logically, the psyche of males is to do everything to gain the favor of women. Men chase them, lust after them, act silly around them, and will do damn near anything to get their attention. Therefore, women are, theoretically, the ultimate focal point of our society.

If you look back at the history of the world, you will learn about the many societies that were created and destroyed by the powerful influences of women. This proves their level of importance. It is undeniable to the rational eye. Take heed.

I think the biggest problem related to this topic is that women have let too much mental abuse to go on for too long, while allowing their abusers to profit by taking what they want without earning it. Women have become weakened by their emotions and have forgotten about their true power. If you are a woman reading this book and are affected by this problem, you must start telling yourself that you have full control over your relationship issues with men, and really believe it. You must not let them come into your world and do whatever they want to do to you. You don't have to give a man a damn thing if you are not ready to. You have to think more for yourself, and seek happiness in that manner. Once you know for certain that you are with a man who deserves everything, then you can give him everything. You can't just give the world to every Tom, Dick, and Harry. If you did, those people wouldn't necessarily feel motivated to work hard to get what you would be giving them. At that point, they would feel that they could do or say anything to you and still get their way. Ladies, you have the power, so use it wisely. You cannot settle just to have a man around.

Some women openly allow no good, second rate men into their lives and still yearn for more quality. They go on to cover up their issues of complacency by saying, "I don't know what's wrong with these men today," and by accepting the low standards they have of men, which only adds to their dismay. The scenario for good, single mothers raising young boys is very similar. Moms, I know you aren't the topic of the book, but I love you and I am not going to leave you out. Many of you are doing a great job with parenting, but you must buck up with your boys. They learn how to manipulate women at early ages, so be strong and do not fold. I know they are your babies but you cannot let them get away with everything. Do not become lazy and let them manipulate you into letting them speak to you in disrespectful ways. They are your children and you must set the tone. I believe that men are the only people who can really teach boys to be men, but you can do your part by teaching your boys how to be honorable people. Again, you are the tone-setter.

That Sex Thing

The most common issue that causes problems between men and women is meaningless sex. Let's face it. People who refrain to abstain know that sex has a tremendous ability to complicate things. Too many people let sex lead their relationships. They don't realize that dating and courtship do not exist for mating and that they actually exist for the purpose of gathering information about that person, so future decisions can be made. You can have two people enjoying their time, while getting to know each other, suddenly fall apart after sex occurring too soon. This can happen for many reasons, but the main reasons for post-sex fallouts are because of both, reasonable and unreasonable expectations.

Victims of post-sex fallouts usually assume that since sex took place, the other person will stick around, care about them, and want to commit. That, my friends, is why the Bible and other works of morality oppose fornication. If we obeyed, we wouldn't have so many problems with single parent homes, teenage pregnancy, AIDS, and promiscuity. Again, I am not going to preach to you, but there are reasons why so many important guidelines, rules, and commandments are in place. They are there to keep us from destroying ourselves. Our problem is that our nature forces us to find ways to abuse most things that we touch, and that is why we suffer.

If you are a person who refrains to abstain, early sex is an issue you should make a decision about. If you are a woman and you know you get attached to men easily after sex, think sincerely about the pros and cons of early sex. Oftentimes, things will not end up in your favor. In most cases, one thing will lead to another, then BANG! Afterwards, the guy usually ends up dodging the girl because she misunderstood the original intentions that he may or may not have had in the first place. He then becomes standoffish because he thinks he may have a stalker on his hands, while the girl is organizing a W.A.M (*Women Against Men)* party to get her frustration off of her chest, and they live happily ever after blah, blah, blah! Trust me folks, it's not worth it. I know from experience.

To eliminate the misunderstandings, you may want to just chill out and wait. I know that it may sound impossible to implement, but friendship, courtship, and marriage are the recommended steps to take towards a fulfilling, committed relationship. If you haven't patterned your relationships in this way, you may want to give this a try and note the result.

Black In the "Daze"

For us boys, it generally did not pay to be smart and show it. During elementary school, being smart definitely was not cool. It seemed like an unspoken rule that flaunting superior intelligence was taboo. It was bizarre, but being smart somehow meant you were too nice or soft. This role made it tough on me, and the other boys who really didn't want to act harder than they were. The majority of us would consistently receive bad grades and get whippings when we got home, but that didn't make a big difference to us. We would act this way, so we could look favorable in the eyes of the prettiest girls in school who happened to like dumb-acting tough guys and popular knuckleheads. At least we thought so. We would even go through all of these actions, knowing that when parent-teacher conference time came around, the bad boy images we used in class would be nowhere to be found.

Once junior high school was in session, I realized that most of the girls were either dating the guys from wealthier families that could afford designer clothes and Air Jordan sneakers, or the drug dealing bad boys who acted up in class and never did their homework. I was neither of those characters. I was poor, and the kids never let me forget that, but I was big enough to kick a little butt when disrespected.

Fights were regular occurrences among the young Black boys at that time. We all felt as though we had something to prove to the world. Some of the boys fought because they wanted to look stronger in the eyes of the girls. Other boys fought to defend their pride. I simply did it because I didn't need daily reminders of my situation to come from mouths of other kids. My mother had divorced my father when I was small, because of his weakness for the drug life, so needless to say, I suffered from a monetary point of view; just as much as most of the other fatherless Black children desiring a complete family circle.

After graduating, I enrolled into a nationally recognized boys high school, and so began my re-education. Things changed immediately for me. There were still the class clowns and high school hard guys who tormented the younger kids, but there was one thing that was not the same. There were no girls to impress. This astonished me. I could be myself and not worry about dressing the best or being popular at this school. It felt like I had a new beginning and finally had a chance to start all over again and decide who I wanted to be, instead of deciding who I wanted to act like. I completely understood the environmental differences. This let me know that everything was not the same everywhere. I then realized that I could change my environment and be the decision maker regarding the type of people I wanted around me.

As my dating life progressed, or flat-lined rather, I began to see more and more that the majority of girls liked bad boys or popular guys with thuggish images. This angered me immensely because I didn't want to have to become someone else again, just to please girls. I felt as though I deserved to be sought after and accepted for who I was.

My looks and personality loudly introduced me as an attractive young man who wanted to be a gentleman and treat females nice, but I couldn't do this because girls viewed being nice as a form of weakness and insecurity. Perplexed by this, I began to slowly hate girls for shunning me, while inviting ignorance into their lives.

As time went on, I shouted countless "I told you so," remarks into the faces of the women who chose men that cheated on them, got them pregnant, and abused them. It was obvious to me that this life was inevitable for the women who allowed it. "They got what they deserved because they didn't choose me," I thought.

When I had become hip to the game, I began breezing through my young life breaking hearts and having little mercy because that was what it seemed females wanted. However, throughout that entire time, I knew what was right and that I was wrong, but was too angry to accept it. To me, yes, all women were bitches and ho's, just like Snoop Doggy Dog said. I was so emotionally driven by this new wave of disrespect that I began to embrace it.

On a broader scale, the hatred between the young men and women in DC had become so bad that females would hardly acknowledge my presence. I could not understand why responses from the kindest compliments I gave came back at me in the form of curse words and attitudes. The hatred spread like a plague. Girls I had played with as a boy acted different and treated me like they never knew me at all. To me, this was like warfare. Boys and girls along with men and women of the same race, acted as if they didn't matter or exist. "How could this be?" I asked myself. "What have I become?" I cried aloud.

Years later, I broke down and became real with myself. I finally accepted the truth, and it was simply that I loved my people, and I wanted peace. I wanted the pain to stop and felt the need to apologize to everyone I had hurt along with everyone who had been hurt by other men. During the time I was going through this,

I did not know what God's plan was for me, but I had allowed myself to be driven far off the path of righteousness.

You see, most young men subconsciously carry the hurt and pain of broken relationships from their earlier years into their early twenties. Situations like this are symbolic, in the sense that those men can either move past the pain and learn from it or dwell in the suffering that lingers. This is a vital part in the sensitive stages of deciding what type of men they desire to become.

One of the major points of my biographical story is to show how women influence the decisions men make. This idea is applied to what kind of cars men drive to the shoes they wear. Though the idea of gaining attraction through material possession is a human characteristic, men seem to have the most trouble with it. By no means does my message suggest that men should blame women for their shortcomings. Instead, it simply serves as a description of the experiences of many men, and goes on to state how influential women are in their lives. There are some, however, who actually do pattern their lives based on observation, intelligence, and introspection. Though few practice these strategies initially, they serve as some of the most honored developmental steps sought after by men.

Since we have such a great population of innovative and strong women of the new millennium who stand up, fight for their rights, and take less abuse from society, we can all help motivate them to redirect their powerful drive in the direction of guiding men away from getting away with murder, by not allowing them to do whatever they want when they please. Women need to be more forceful with men who are lacking, by not allowing them to feel that they can achieve their goals with women by using the same weak and effortless advances they have been getting away with.

Ladies and Gentlemen, I suggest that we lead our brothers and sisters to a place that urges them to understand that issues such as unwanted single parenthood and abuse do not have to be an option, and neither does the destruction of the African American community.

Women: It is time for you to respect yourself more and put your foot down in the right place. Do not let men continue to mistreat you, but don't forget to grant the access for the right treatment to come from the right people.

Men: We need to give our women more room to help us get to the place we need to be, not by ourselves, but with our women. It is obvious that we are going to have to do this together because it *ain't* working out on our own. Also fellas, women aren't necessarily angels either, so make sure you understand the type of positive treatment you want to receive from them. Trust me, some of them can become very lacking and lazy too.

What Is Most Important?

Appeal is not equal to importance, but what is important always carries appeal in the long run.

It is a horrible thing to view arrogant people in noticeable positions, bragging about being thugs, having been to jail, and getting shot. What kind of glory do these people think they are gaining by doing such things? Who wants to be a professional thug or gangster, and is there such a thing? If so, do those positions come with good healthcare and pension plans? The dictionary definition for thug is: *A cutthroat or ruffian; a hoodlum.* From this simple description, you and I can assume that living a life as a thug involves some type of violence or wrong doing, and is rewarded by jail time or execution. In my opinion, whoever would rather a quick thug life over an honest life that provides happiness, intelligence, and longevity, is a fool. I know that it is harder for Black people in less fortunate societies to achieve their goals, but everyone has the option of being a good or a not so good person. To not try is the same as failure. There is no excuse.

On that note, what is it with women liking bad guys who do nothing to promote their futures with those women? I remember the days when women begged for sensitive men who would treat them right and love them better. Today, sensitive men are in the back seat, coming in last place. Who's driving though? Aha! You've got it. Confused women, that's who.

I don't know how sensitive I am, but I do know how to treat a woman, and to be honest, treating a woman well just doesn't work sometimes. I'm not talking about buying her things either. Look at it this way, a woman has to be able to accept something that a man is giving or offering to her in order for that woman to acknowledge the gift and be happy with it. Therefore a woman who is unhappy with herself and who is blinded by her own issues would more than likely, not be able to see the goodness that a particular man may be trying to display to her. In turn, all men, instead of some men, would be made out to be careless, cheap, and lacking in the chivalry department because of the deficiency of goodness that the woman sees. Situations like these are not good for the confidence of young Black men who work hard to catch the attention of Black women all over.

This issue ties over into jobs and other material possessions that should not be idolized. There is absolutely nothing wrong with a woman having the goal of marrying a doctor or an architect, but there is something wrong with a woman who will not entertain thoughts of being with a man who works as a plumber, social worker, or teacher. The ironic thing about this is that the men who work those jobs may be the good men women claim do not exist. Therefore, those men are judged and overlooked. Once again, where is our focus? Some women just won't give those guys the time of day, and that is 100% wrong. Why are things this way? Is it the embarrassment that comes from the fact that those men have shameful professions, or is it that they aren't flashy enough?

What I would like you to see and believe is that neither men nor women are perfect. We all have our hang-ups and issues, and the elimination of those concerns should be our main concern. Also, we need to get rid of our constant urges to design our mates. We should not be picky, but must aspire to be intelligently selective instead. Such requirements ranging from skin color, having no kids, and being tall enough, to the number of owned vehicles and dinners purchased should not be our focus. Whether working as postmen, teachers, or secretaries, our Black men should be judged by their worth, and qualities equally.

Simple Mistakes Women Make

It is my understanding that there are no such things as bad people. To me, people sometimes do bad things. Unsuccessful dating experiences don't reveal that two people cannot be successful together. It merely shows evidence of misguidance and the mistakes that come of it. One of the many problems that misguided women make is that they sometimes prioritize their goals, regarding men, in disastrous ways. The dilemma is not that some women don't know what they want. It is that they are unaware of what is really important. Most women definitely know what is appealing to them. That is clear, but the question that follows is,

"Is appeal equal to importance?" Another question I have for women who value long lasting relationships is, "What is the most important, long term characteristic of the man you envision loving to the end?" Since longevity is the key, I believe in this way of thinking and suggest that it be used. Remember, "Appeal is not equal to importance, but what is important always carries appeal in the long run."

There are several suggestions about personal goals, values, and characteristics being the main tools for the selection of a partner in this book. These references propose a framework, and introduce strategic patterns that could potentially lead couples to relationship success. I believe that the seeker must first have his or her own preferences about their ideal partner's personality. In addition, this person should study his own objective in order to make sure those desires are realistically attainable. Your decision should be based, in part on your expectations of a relationship you view as being favorable.

To gain further insight, figure out what he or she wants from life. Talk about your dreams, hobbies, and goals, in addition to religious, and political beliefs. These days, many relationships end prematurely because partners allow the relationship to grow without first discussing these topics. Instead of looking in all of the right places, they look in all of the wrong places. If you are not sure about the difference, read this passage again and ask yourself, "Am I looking in the right place?" Adapting to this frame of mind will allow you to make better decisions and help you bring happiness and success to the life of your relationship.

Six

How To Find and Keep A Good Black Man

"Take heed, and keep your soul diligently, lest you forget the things which your eyes have seen, and lest they depart from your heart all the days of your life; make them known to your children and your children's children."

Deuteronomy 4:9

"Where is the good Black Man?" Sadly, many people ask this question because they feel they do not have the answer. Some would have you believe that he doesn't exist. "All of our Black men are dead, locked up, gay, or on the down low," many claim. It is very upsetting to know that Black women believe this more than most. That belief, however, comes from the loss of hope and aspiration regarding positive relationships. It is additionally disappointing to be faced with the awareness of the fact that groups of Black women have been affected by the world's view on Black men, and have been hurt so much by way of failed relationships, that they have given up on the search.

Don't Believe the Hype

Good Black men are everywhere

When it comes to exaggerated ideas about the location of good Black men, there have been quite a lot of voiced references and statements that just aren't true. The reality of the situation is nothing less than catastrophic for good Black men. The Up High man's point of view disproves the message of the people who proclaim that most Black men in America are dead, homosexual, or in jail. Unfortunately, we African Americans are in a stage of crisis as a people and must unite. However, if you believe most of our men are unavailable because they are dead, incarcerated, gay, or on the down low, you have been severely misled. Yes, there is a disproportional percent of African American men who are incarcerated and are not college graduates. Yes, the female to male ratio in schools and chocolate cities all over the United States may be statistically discouraging, but don't believe the hype. Stop torturing yourself over the numbers and think realistically about the cause and solution. Yes, the number of female college graduates has long surpassed that of males since the 1970s most recent male lead, and yes, many male high school graduates go into the military or straight into the work force rather than attending college. It hurts me to answer yes to these questions, but in no way, shape, or form does my answer reflect that most Black men are unsuccessful, lazy, drug-dealing people who are unable to speak correctly. Truly, there are people who would like for you to believe that though. Let us not forget that this country looks down on Blacks and always has. Therefore, it should not be surprising to notice the pitfalls that have been placed in front of our feet, as a people. Though this is true, it is without excuse that this is our reality. It makes me wonder if there is anyone who really believes that America's Black male really gets a fair shake in this 'equal' society of ours.

Look at our history, folks. This type of trickery dates back to times like the Civil War, when this country began using slaves in combat roles. The African American community also paid a disproportionately high price in Vietnam, where one out of five servicemen was Black. Many of those men who died would have been marriage prospects for our women today. Did you ever think about that?

Why is it that the minority races are recruited more than the majority race? Aren't there more of them anyway? According to the government's census data, Blacks only represent 12% of this country's population, which is a lie. If they can deceive millions in a presidential election, what makes you think that the ones in power are not manipulating the displayed ratio of Black U.S. citizens?

The American Council has attributed the large drop in Black college enrollment to the intense military recruiting of minorities. How could this be? How can Americans allow the majority of military recruiting to take place in areas of mass minority and low income? Statistics show that many soldiers who die on the front lines are Black and Latino kids who join the army, and are sent to fight and die. Also, People of color represent one-third of all personnel but only one-eighth of that third are officers. It is also a fact that only 35% of recruits successfully receive any education benefits from the military. I hope that tells you something.

Mainstream media outlets like the government, education directors, and anti-Black organizations do everything they can to manipulate the world into smiling upon their kind and looking down on Blacks. What have Blacks done to deserve this hatred? Is it the fact that slaves were the ones who built this country during the four hundred years plus slavery era, or the fact that Blacks didn't want to be slaves anymore that created this hatred? There are people who are glad that our men and women are in turmoil right now. Those same people would like to hurt us and have us kill each other, rather than give us any credit. Our separation was constructed by design. We didn't just grow apart as a people. Slave masters separated Black families from the beginning, because they knew that an estranged people could not succeed as a unified group. Many leaders of our American societies do anything and everything they can to force their negative images onto the Black man. It is up to us to make a great stand to force the truth into consideration. This will clear away most of the negative stigma that pins the Black man's defiled image against the wall.

A great strategy that both men and women should implement in hopes of reconnecting the good Black man and the good Black woman, is to realize what is real and what is not, regarding our views of one another. We must have realistic expectations as a people. We should be aware that not one relationship in this world has ever been perfect and that it is okay to stumble. Getting back up is the hard part, but is also the most beneficial.

Everyone has had one or many situations in their relationships that have not gone their way, but this does not make it acceptable to create negative stereotypes and irrational generalizations pointed directly at an entire gender of any particular race. Unsupported stereotypes can never realistically compete with the purity of rationality.

We should also remind ourselves that new relationships force us to make small gambles by inviting new people into our intimate spaces, while naturally giving them a certain amount of trust. The undeniable truth is this: sometimes you win and sometimes you lose, but let us not forget about the times where losing may not be losing at all. Either way you look at it, relationships are never perfect because we as individuals are not perfect. In order for a relationship to be perfect, it would need to have not one, but two perfect people at the helm. This is impossible to accomplish, however, I do propose the idea that two individuals can be perfect for one another and can manage to deal with each other's faults as best as they can. Maintaining such a relationship would require hard work from both parts.

When it comes to playing inside the world of success, it is understood that winning and losing go hand in hand. They are actually inseparable. Every champion has lost at some point in the game. It is about how they handled the loss that mattered. Instead of pouting or quitting, a true winner knows how to lose and learn from the results of the loss. When speaking of relationships, that is my way of describing a winning attitude, and we must have winning attitudes if we want to create good, long lasting relationships. Women must have winning attitudes in order to see and appreciate the Up High man who walks up and down the street, just as the rest of us do. This is necessary for our continued survival.

The Search

A woman who has little to no knowledge about what to look for in a good man will more than likely not recognize him. If she does not recognize him, then he might as well be extinct.

The act of finding the good Black man seems to be the most discussed enigma boggling the minds of many of today's Black women. Many ask, "How do I find a good Black man?" I'll start off by saying, "The good Black man cannot be found, because he is not missing." Perhaps people have lost their focus, causing their vision to become blurred, rendering them incapable of recognizing what is real and what is not; what is good and what is bad.

In my eyes, not being able to identify good men seems to have become a horrific problem for women throughout America, but on the other hand, I really don't believe that an average group of women would be able to recognize a good man if he showed up on a lottery ticket. However, I also believe that the true location of good Black men is very clear to others who feel the need to ask the question about the Black man's whereabouts. These are just thoughts, but let's go in deeper for a closer look, shall we?

The idea of being missing or misplaced has done much damage to the reign of good men and it must be stopped. If you are a Black woman who believes that the good Black man is extinct, ask yourself, "Where is my focus?" Also, inquire within and ask, "Am I being realistic in my judgment, and am I doing everything possible to ensure that my insecurities aren't clouding my judgment?" I think many women should question whether they honestly believe there are no good men around. It is very important for women to be as realistic and honest as possible with regard to the search for good men.

Often times, multitudes of unrealistic women yearn to discover the latitude and longitude coordinates of that mythical place called 'Good Man Island'. They can forget about that though, because it's just not going to happen. My theory is that women cross paths with good men every day, but may not realize it. Those women don't take situational instances into account that would not allow them to understand why they are not seizing the moments that may pass them by daily. Dr Phil's thoughts explain how, for some women, it may be an inconceivable way of thinking to understand that they often are often faced with opportunities to meet good, compatible men. The lack of good identification and recognition methods for locating those men plays a huge role in the occurrences of sightlessness that take place. It may strike many with disbelief to hear that they may be regularly passing up on those opportunities for several reasons. Some of the causes that generate those instances occur because of several difficult-to-notice issues that stem from anger, denial, insecurity, distraction, and lack of confidence. Those feelings along with so many others, have the power of handicapping its carrier, and that has become part of the problem, not the solution.

It is essential that we realize and accept that good Black men are not missing, nor have they been placed on anyone's endangered species list. Believe it or not, he is right under our noses. When we are on the street, he is on the sidewalk. When we are in the store, mall, or library, he is there as well. If you really want to exercise your mind a little, think about the fact that he is even in church on Sunday, praising God for giving him the strength to be the good Black man that he is. Self-preparation would allow women to notice him more and would prove to him that those women are worthy of his goodness as well.

Good Black men have emotions and believe that they possess precious qualities that should be respected, just as women do. They don't feel that they are above any other person, but do believe that women, like men, do have to prove themselves to some degree. In addition to that, I think it should be the goal of African American women everywhere, to uplift every Black man they know who is doing a great job at being a good Black man. I make this suggestion because of what I wrote earlier. "Good Black men have emotions, want to feel appreciated, and need that feedback." It is human nature to desire appreciation and want to work hard to please others, when rewarded. It sounds like a win-win situation to me.

Aim High and Never Settle For Less

The minute you settle for less than you deserve, you get even less than you settle for.

Settling for less is a disease that paralyzes many of us who lack the courage or hope to change things for the better. A lot of times, women allow men to come into their lives, treat them like crap, and get the best of them, because they don't believe they will find anything better. This is why settling must not be an option. It provides a clear pathway directly to relationship suicide. Women in these situations usually sacrifice their happiness, because of the little faith in their ability to have and keep good men. This is not a good way to think because having little to no faith hardly ever promotes success. However, this is a problem that can be fixed by increasing faith in God, who is the key to every single thing in and outside of life. I know that talks of God and spirituality can bring about very broad and moral conversations, so to avoid that, I have found a way to sum it up in two easy steps, so bear with me. Step one is the cause and step two is the effect. The good thing about implementing these steps is that you don't have to pay $19.99 for them. Are you ready?

Step 1(The Cause): Increase your faith in God. Walk in his shadow, and make your relationship with Him personal and intimate. Stay on the path he paves and pray that His will be done for you and not that your will be done for yourself.

Step 2(The Effect): Your faith in a relationship with a good heterosexual Black man will increase. I promise.

Let me warn you, though. When you are dealing with our Father,

God, things don't always happen exactly when you want them to. They happen if and when they are supposed to, so be patient. The funny thing about people is that we always want to shout out when we think we are ready for something to happen in our lives. Anyway, the point is that our viewpoints are limited far past our abilities of knowledge or expression. Most of us don't even know what our purpose on this planet is, and if you don't know that, then how could your plan be better than the plan of the omnipresent being that created your tail in the first place?" Our masterful God places things in front of us when we can handle them. Not when it will break us. Sometimes he'll do what you want just to teach you a lesson, which lets you know that you weren't as ready as you thought you were.

Another issue that we people have is that we often lose sight of our goals. When this happens, the plans or steps that a person would normally take to reach those goals utterly fade away. My suggestion towards fighting against the idea of our human forgetfulness and laziness is to incorporate a pyramid-like system of static operation, which would support certain sequential levels of significance and value. Level one of my personal pyramid involves my spirituality and belief in God, as they both drive and motivate my desire for righteousness. Give it a try.

A wise woman once wrote to me stating, "The primary emphasis toward companionship should be God." She also said, "You should seek God before searching for a mate." I concur, but who does that anymore? She continued to write, "Both men and women should ask him for wisdom and patience in order to weed people out of their lives who aren't good for them." Honestly, I believe that this should be a prerequisite for all things we do in life. After building that primary, guiding level of your pyramid, you can slowly and effectively begin creating other areas that stem from its essence. It is up to you to design your pyramid the best way for you, so you can be successful in reaching your goal of happiness.

I love God with all of my heart and get excited about his plan, but you can relax, knowing that I am not going to preach to you today. Instead, I want you to understand that my opinion does not suggest that an atheist cannot find a good man or woman; however, the truth of the matter is that one has to believe in something in order to achieve anything. In this case, the ultimate success comes through God's will, which is everlasting. That is what we should be aiming for. A good example of this could be one's belief in him or her self. If that belief is not present, then complacency will exist and confidence will not. Belief is an essential part of attaining anything, and without it, failure is imminent.

Ladies, please have faith in our men. If you are doing the things I suggested, in regard to aiding your preparation, you should rest assured, knowing you will be ready to be swept away when that good man arrives at your doorstep. Don't believe the hype. Even if the numbers are skewed, do not settle. If you have children, teach them not just to be cautious of bad people, but to be aware of the good Black men that exist as well. Show them the glory of Black men and tell them how important they are to us. Also, teach them what you know to be true of the man with whom you hold love and desire, so their generation may have better connection between Black men and women.

Don't Let Love Lead the Way

I have found that many people make the mistake of placing entirely too much emphasis on the guidance of love in their relationships by making it the foundation. Wrong! Unfortunately, what they sometimes do, in their effort to keep their partners, is place commitment before compatibility.

I think of love as an entity that does whatever it wishes, with anyone allowing its entrance. It does not consider things rationally or intelligently, like we try to do. You should not let love lead you without thinking. If you do, then you might end up with a broken heart.

Governing your relationships by allowing love to take over would create a perfect setting for failure. When it comes to issues of the heart, we have absolutely no say when love is our guide. We try, but wielding the power of love is impossible. Many have attempted, but they have failed. The hard part is having the understanding of all of this, and realizing that love is a tool. It is a very powerful tool, but nonetheless, it is a tool. It allows itself to be used, but not controlled. Therefore, all you have to do is point it in the right direction and let intelligence and God's guidance do the rest. I say this because the decision for a mate should be made on a spiritual and intellectual basis before it's made on an emotional one. Before pursuing a relationship with someone, you should acquire clearance from God, review his attributes of commitment, and allow your heart to engage. Whatever you do, do not let your emotions take steps before you do.

Relationships Are Not as Easy as They Seem

Something we all must understand about the game of love is that relationships require hard work sided by devotion and determination. Also, since we can never reach perfection in anything we do, we should keep reminding ourselves that there is no such thing as a perfect relationship. Perfection is what television presents, but it is not real. People do not get married and live happily ever after. Although reading this may discourage your hopes of blissful perfection, I hope you remain encouraged enough to know that our blessing reflects the reality that we can still try to reach perfection. There is nothing shameful about having the goal of reaching perfection, while knowing you will never fully grasp it. After all, what is life without hope? What is God without faith? That is exactly what a goal is. Too many people have unreasonable views of relationships being circumstances of flawlessness and happiness with another person. They don't take time to understand that there will always be bumps in the road. Those people should know, however, that the more realistic conclusion delivers the reality that, when those bumps do come, you and your partner will have the choice to smooth those bumps out. Nothing in relationships will ever be perfect, but you can make things as perfect as possible with the person that is perfect for you.

Prepare Yourself

Knowing that he was a good man and that he wanted to be married someday, Mark worked diligently to refine himself in preparation for the possibilities of what was to come. Mark knew that marriage was an important bond and that it took tons of work and dedication. While waiting to find that special someone, he decided that he would improve himself by increasing his values and potentially virtuous characteristics. Mark wisely put his patience, communication, and consideration qualities to the test. He knew that no successful relationship would last without good communication. He also was aware that a lack of patience often opened doors for quick tempers and anger, and that using the proper doses of consideration could put out the biggest fires or become the sweetest icing on any cake.

So, in essence, Mark knew that every relationship had its problems, but he wanted to get a head start on the usual causes of problematic occurrences by working on eliminating issues that he may have possibly brought to the table before. This was his way of wanting to spend more time having good experiences instead of awkward moments that could be crucial early on.

This brings us back to the topic of this chapter. The most important answer to the highly controversial question of how to find and keep a good man is to prepare oneself. Properly preparing for any goal is the surest way of predicting what is to come, in addition to controlling it effectively. If you somehow found something you wanted but were not prepared for, the chances of you keeping it would be very slim, right? The wise decision should always be to ready yourself before its arrival, in order to guarantee its stay within your grasp. For that reason, the question should not be, "How do I find a good Black man?" The questions should be, "How do I prepare myself," "What do I do when I find him," and finally, "What will I do to keep him, once I have him?"

Primarily, a woman should be absolutely clear that she really wants and can handle a partner. She can do so by creating quality reasons for finding a partner by asking, "Why do I really want a man?" She should then study her answers and take time to eliminate or reposition the levels of her goals by importance if she finds that her reasons are a little off. For example, some women may need assistance with bills or may need help putting food on the table. Those are both acceptable desires, but are those desires rational reasons for entering a relationship with a man? I don't think so, because a man in that situation would be getting low-balled from the beginning. On the other hand, longing for companionship and someone to care for are both two great *relational* reasons for creating a bond.

My overall advice to women is to not place too much emphasis on finding a man. Instead, focus on making yourself a better individual. Allow life to take place naturally, without interference, and don't set superficial standards that your potential suitor may not be able to meet.

In order to find their soul mate, single men and women of every age should take great initiative in preparing themselves mentally and physically. If your goal is to be in a long lasting relationship, you should get to know yourself first. Become intimate with your life's goals and your values. You should learn to embrace who you are and love yourself before attempting to find love in another. Remind yourself that, in a relationship, there is no 'us' before there is 'me.'

If you are a woman who has been hurt by a man, the goal should be for you to get the healing process started and move forward as quickly as your emotions will allow. This should be done to ensure that a future suitor would not suffer from the effects of past relationship failures. These helpful suggestions do not only pertain to intimate relationships, they will help in virtually all kinds of relationships. Think of them as an investment and remind yourself that an investment in self is as good as an investment in all of your relationships. Be smart about things. Instead of jumping into another dysfunctional relationship, arm yourself with sensible relationship preparation tools and strategies that will benefit you. If you had bad luck in the past with determining the rate of compatibility for you and your partner, you should now make it a point not to place commitment before compatibility. You and your partner should be sure that you both are like-minded and well matched before pursuing anything serious. The mistake many people make is that they place commitment first and suffer later because of it. Compatibility should always be your primary objective. Make sure that you and your potential mate have many goals and values in common, and that your personalities complement each other. I'm not talking about you both having an appreciation for movies or food. I am speaking of you matching your characteristics and ideas. Begin your next relationship from a position of assurance, good intention, and self-respect.

Another very important thing a woman should focus on in order for her process of preparation to work effectively, is to make sure she knows what qualities she wants in a man, as well as what she wants from that man. Scores of unprepared women jump into relationships without even knowing what they want, so consequently, they tend to get what they don't want or can't handle. This is what I call self-sabotage. In this case, the woman loses the battle before it even begins. An equally important approach is for her to make sure she knows what she does not want in and from a man. This plan also works well for men seeking women.

In terms of reference, it has been inspiring to discover from a religious prospective, how many of the answers to the prayers we seek, concerning relationships, are presented in the *Bible.* Even if you are not Christian, I am sure that the teachings offered within the book's pages would still give meaning to your search for patience and perseverance. What better place is there to look than to the most studied book of all time? I have used the *Bible* as a reference tool for my life, because I knew that if I followed its teachings and feared its warnings, my problems in life would become smaller. Speaking specifically about compatibility, the Bible verse 6:14, from the second book of *Corinthians* reads, "Be ye not unequally yoked together with unbelievers; for what fellowship hath righteousness with unrighteousness and what communion hath light with darkness?" We have to be equally yoked for the union that we yearn for.

Taking a gamble with this one will not work. Compatibility is the key. Find it and use it.

Having Similar Goals Helps

Goals are very important in relationships and generally, the chance that comes from taking relationship gambles increases when he has goals similar to yours, ladies. For example, if you know you want to be married with a family and home in a nice suburban area, it probably would not be a good idea to make too many future plans with a man who speaks disrespectfully to his mother and works the corner on the block. It is a good likelihood that his family values and career goals, or lack there of, may interfere with the achievement of your dreams.

Women, go and figure out the types of goals and values you want to hear your potential mate speak about. Ask him questions directly or let time help fill you in as you go along. You may want to ask him what he thinks the best strategies are, for solving arguments and disagreements. Ask him about his feelings toward communication, consideration, and compromise. Don't ignore warning signs, potential problems, or issues of concern. Ask him about his vision and goals. Is his life guided by senses of ambition and purpose, or does he just allow life to take place around him? What is his sense of family orientation like? Who are his friends and what are they like? Does he have a good level of patience?

Walking similar walks and having like opinions on general, every day issues are what you should be looking for in your relationship with your man. How much do the two of you have in common? Do each of your talents and blessings compliment his, and vice versa? Do your goals for the future match up? Have the both of you effectively established yourselves as a team, so you can battle those everyday issues of concern together? Chris Jackson explains this in the "*Beyond Dinner and a Movie*" chapter of his book entitled *The Black Christian Singles Guide to Dating and Sexuality*. He wrote about creative conversation topics that women usually want to ask men about, but never really do. Questions and suggestions that Mr. Jackson presents cover a wide variety of issues ranging from that special someone's favorite color, to family matters. There are several topics we should really think about and discuss with one another, so the levels of surprise that we may encounter can be kept to a small degree. If you are doing all of these things, ladies, then you have already either found that good man or are on your way.

Going To Church May Not Be Enough

This is an issue that women should be very careful with. One thing that we must understand is that many people who attend church do it for positive, spiritual fellowship. That reality is a beautiful thing, but we also have to make room for the church hawks and perpetrating soul predators lurking in the mist. Church hawks are people who attend church for reasons outside of spirituality. Their attendance involves reasons like meeting men or women, gossiping, and competing with fashion and dress. Let me break it down for you. Most religions are composed of a certain set of beliefs that define their devotion. Christianity uses the church as a worship place to feed our spiritual ideal. Many people get the church's purpose confused with spirituality. They wake up on Sunday morning, pop their gospel CD in, put their fancy clothes on, and go to church. To them, this is all they think they need to achieve in order for their spirit to be fed. They may not understand that worshiping God has nothing to do with their dress or style. They may not realize that the biggest church hats will not get them into heaven. They also may not be able to comprehend how running around the altar, shouting the loudest unknown tongue may get them into hell faster than not going to church at all. You see, a church is a place where people are supposed to worship God. Most people lose sight of that and use their time in church to socialize. They forget that God is not a church; he is church. It is my opinion that focusing on spirituality is more profitable to a true believer than just going to church one day a week. That is why many churchgoers lose track of their goals. A highly spiritual person may listen to gospel music throughout the week and pray several times throughout the day because that is what they believe keeps them on the path of righteousness. Others cheat and deny their lazy, uncommitted nature later. They don't need Sunday morning to transform themselves into saints.

So, when a woman wants to know if a man is led by God, she should ask about his spirituality, and not about how much he goes to church. She should be specific about her desire to know about that man's faith. I myself, truthfully exclaim that I don't have perfect church attendance, but I have been asked about it and have been judged because of it. A few of those times, the women who asked scowled at me like I was a demon. What they did was judge my level of spirituality based off of how much they thought I went to church. On the flipside, if they would have asked me about my sense of spirituality or about my relationship with God, they might not have been able to shut me up. This strategy suggests a better way of communicating, which will allow you to get exactly what you want. It gives the other person the chance to explain him or herself, rather than give them the opportunity to blurt a one-word answer like, "Yes."

Women who value spirituality in their men also may not want to pursue men who are hesitant or unsure about their levels of spirituality. Get a good understanding about who he is and what he desires by asking him the right questions the right way. Seek the information that you need in order to know what you will accept and what you won't. Being direct is important and does have its advantages.

Pay Close Attention To His Words and Actions

Believe it or not, many men often say exactly what they want and don't want to occur in relationships. It is also a fact that, sometimes women have that disease called selective hearing, which doesn't allow them to know what the man is feeling until a later discussion or argument. If you have a problem like this, take the time to look far past the obvious winning characteristics that your potential suitor possesses, and do some surface level investigation. This will give you the chance to get a closer look inside, and it is a very wise approach to understanding your counterpart.

For some women, seeing that a guy has a nice car, is successful, and attractive is all they need to know before making big decisions about the future. They sometimes feel as though they will work with what they have and change the rest of him as they go along. Newsflash! That will not work.

Lesson number one is that you can't change people, because they change themselves. People don't just up and alter their personalities, because someone else decides it is necessary. For example, if a man says he isn't interested in a relationship and the woman he is dating has the desire for a relationship, then it would be best for her to respectively decline and keep on searching. Equally so, if the man doesn't want to marry and she does, then she should not waste her time living in a state of denial.

If you are a sister who has trouble with these issues, you might want to start listening to what your man is saying. Make an attempt at reality. Just take his word for it and let him go. Trust me, you will be happy later. His expressed feelings and answers can either confirm positive feelings he has for you, or save you a lot of time and emotion.

Another great way for a woman to enhance her judgment by way of analysis, is to take a look at the types of relationships the man has with his family and friends. Everybody knows that birds of a feather flock together, but most women look past the importance of uncovering what kinds of people are interwoven in the most intimate circles of their men. How does he treat his mother? What are his morals and personality characteristics telling you? Does his family have an abusive past? Has he been exposed to alcoholism or drugs? If you are a woman, who has not studied these important characteristics, you may want to start now, by doing some further investigation. Remember that taking an in-depth look at a man's inner circle, in most cases, reveals the mold from which he was cast.

Make Sure Your Expectations Are Realistic

The downfall of many women is that they have quite a few unrealistic expectations of men and unfortunately, when those particular expectations aren't met; men are judged and labeled improperly. Without expecting perfection, women should still strive to be perfect and go after the next best thing, being what is perfect for them. That involves getting to know their personalities and characteristics well enough to be able to tell the difference. This way, unrealistic expectations will transform into realistic actions, which will better the chances for more fruitful relationships.

Over the years, women have cried out for the types of men they thought they needed. The macho men of the early 80s were urged to focus on their looks and style, while the late 80s and early 90s introduced the need for more emotional, soft men with sensitivity. When that didn't work, the thuggish man became the desires of many confused women. Can somebody say 'contradiction?' Like I said before, men will do whatever women want, because women ultimately pave the way. They just have to make up their minds about what they really want and need.

Primarily, women must create reasonable goals regarding the features and idiosyncrasies of their men. Those goals should be well rounded and should include positive mental and physical characteristics that compliment the woman's own. No one is perfect, not even the Up High so much that it turns into them only accepting what they think is perfect, instead of what is perfect for them or what they need. What they misunderstand is that 'want' and 'need' are two different things. Want is usually a desire that a person can live without. Need happens to be something that one must have to complete their incompletion. Not to say that a woman needs a man to complete her personality or life, but she does need the quality necessities that a man can provide to be ultimately content. My example of contentment references a heterosexual woman, faced with the option of having a good man or not. We all can assume that she would rather not pass by the good man, as his presence would give her satisfaction. The strong Black woman knows this and is not ashamed to say, "I need a good man," nor is the strong Black man ashamed to say the same about a woman.

The truth about this topic is that expectations are always existent. Most times, we really do have the full intent of wanting to receive something from someone. No matter how small or large, we all have certain expectations. Realistically speaking, we should always talk about most of our expectations with the person that we are involved with. I know that most may view that as taboo, but it is a great way to communicate and create trust.

Now That You've Got Him, Keep Him

Women, in order to keep the Up High man that you have always wanted, you must make sure you provide a comfortable environment for him to love you in. You can start by doing things like sharing and supporting his dreams without losing sight of your own. This is a good way of doing things, because common interests not only bring people together, they help keep people together. Men living on the Up High love to have partners who not only value their dreams and goals, but also support and contribute to them. This brings a feeling of togetherness and companionship that both partners want very much. In turn, he will reciprocate tenfold.

Help him express his true feelings and learn to better the expression of your own. Be patient with this because it may take some time. Keep at it though, because the outcome provides a better platform for communication overall. Work with him in order to produce a healthy level of compromise, but stick to your principles. Be strong in your reasoning, but remain pure at heart when listening to his. Stand your ground with your decisions, but at the same time, know that you are not the only one with an opinion. Continue by encouraging him, and do not nag. He will love you for it.

Women, as good partners, are usually instrumental in helping men find their paths and purposes. This is an extraordinary ability of the woman that good men all over the world cherish. Those women take the time to become interested in the lives and passions of their men. They make it a point to give advice and encouragement that is beneficial to the man's happiness and success. This is a good example of teamwork and union between couples.

Nurture Your Relationship

Here are a few suggestions for women who consider the desires and happiness of good men enough to feel that those good men should be made to feel special:

• Tell him of your attraction to him and show appreciation for what he believes in as well as what he does, so his confidence in being a leader remains firm.

We, men, don't need much, ladies, but we do need something. Almost anything counts, but, honestly, everyone wants to feel special in the eyes of another. Giving this to our men will help them feel desire and appreciation from you as well as boost their confidence and trust for you.

• Show appreciation and gratitude for the things he does, for you and your relationship.

During dates in the past, a woman telling me how much she had enjoyed herself always made me feel good and satisfied. I believe that any man who cares about a woman's comfort would be happy to hear the same. Anything good, presented by you about the time you spend together is golden. If you nurture him and show him appreciation, you are ultimately investing by securing respect and building trust.

• Don't hesitate to ask him for help.

Men like to feel like they are experts on certain topics. Anything that is manly is usually the content of those topics, so ask him about his assistance pertaining to electronics, your vehicle, things around the house, or whatever. Doing this also presents you to be in a position of humility, which can make your mate feel more accepted and useful.

• Express a healthy amount of heartfelt interest in something he likes to be a part of individually, or with you.

This could include sports or outings with his friends or family. He may like it if you take some sort of interest in his hobbies or volunteer work. Remember to be sincere with your consideration. Pretending will only get you somewhere you do not want to be.

• Help make a deserving man feel good. Cook for him from time to time and Give him his favorite dessert, whatever that may be.

Again, this only pertains to the men who deserve this preferred treatment. Not everybody is worthy of the pleasures that only a real woman can provide. Ladies, I know that most of you think you are already doing enough to please your man, and some of your men would probably agree, but there is never an end to ideas when it comes to pleasing a man. Yes, cooking, hypothetically, is the way to a man's heart. Some sisters do it and many others don't. The ones that don't and won't, however, are usually the ones that should not be complaining about not finding a good catch. Maybe they have been around the ones who hadn't deserved it. Who knows? The man who proves his worth through his actions should receive the things he desires from time to time, because he too, is a prize.

Communication Is Essential

Communication is the art and technique of using words effectively to pass on and accept information or ideas. It is a very important tool of expression that we all use to collectively interact. Since proper communication is so vital, I believe that words, sided with their exact definitions, play a major role in the understanding of statements that are exchanged between people. Because we, as African Americans are so creative with everything we do, we often use our creativity to alter meanings of words that already have definitions. This sometimes causes communication confusion within our own culture, which leads people to have conflicting views of how to relate certain words or messages into their lifestyles. Take dating for instance. For some, dating is an open, polygamous status used by people with goals of ultimately seeing one person, and for others it involves only two people. Many people feel that a date means going out with the opposite sex, no matter whether they are strictly friends or more than that. Others believe that it only involves persons with whom they hold interest. What is your definition of dating, and would you feel comfortable with effectively communicating that definition to a potential companion?

To eliminate most of the communication confusion that we sometimes find ourselves buried in, we should aspire to tactically deliver words that mean exactly what we feel, in addition to asking questions with the goal of receiving the exact kind of answer we require for understanding. This would help eliminate assumptions and suspicion of deceit.

Time and time again, I have listened to women explain how they had no expectations of our dating relationships, without regard to the true definition of the word 'expectation.' Because of that, I disagreed and felt that those women communicated the wrong idea instead of being honest. As an exemplary tool of reason, I will explain this point another way.

On a fist date, I expect the woman to dress attractively enough to stimulate me. I hold that same ideal for myself. If her hair is not dressed properly, or if her nail polish is heavily chipped, those things, alone, will tell me where her priorities are, how she views herself, and how much she considers my opinion. The bottom line is that nobody wants a lazy partner who does nothing to please him or her. Consideration is a very important level of communication that all relationship seekers should pay attention to and support. It could make things that much better.

The Challenge

The first step in being a leader is knowing the honor in being a servant.

I propose a challenge to anyone who is man or woman enough to face imperfection within themselves, while welcoming a productive attitude of teamwork into their lives that will speak *success* into existence. Put your down your pride and get rid of your ego. Winning is not worth losing that person who brings happiness to your life and relationship. I also challenge you to learn from your mistakes and move forward, knowing that the next situation will be better. Also, create a game plan. Get to know yourself and figure out what specific characteristics, values, and qualities you think you want in a potential companion. Prepare yourself for the possibility of being in a successful relationship with that person. Once you've done that, sit down and choose what types of characteristics you would not be happy with in a potential companion. By accepting good values and qualities and by eliminating bad ones, I guarantee improvement in your dating experiences. I refer to this as the process of replacing the bad with the good.

When finished with these steps, you should have a greater understanding of what is best for you, and you will then be well on your way to witnessing more successful dating experiences first hand.

Seven

Interracial Relationships

"Injustice anywhere is a threat to justice everywhere"
Dr. Martin Luther King Jr.

Interracial relationships between Black and White men and women have always been problematic for some. However, society's stance toward such associations has come a very long way since the end of segregation. Most issues relating to these relationships were initially born out of the racial and social gap between Whites and Blacks. Because of this, today many Black women sneer at the sight of interracial couples. Those same Black women often have the tendency to view the men in those situations as traitors. These instances have occurred many times throughout America's history, but the generalized judgment of all interracial relationships is immoral.

When referencing interracial relationships between Whites and Blacks, our history shows us that the still young liberty of slaves has come very far, and things are changing dramatically. This was part of Dr. King's dream. We are all God's people, and it is far past time when we should have begun to behave like it.

Our freedom from segregation for less than forty years along with the knowledge of how things have changed should make us conscious of how America's views on White and Black heterosexual relationships should be more accepted. There are many reasons why the opposers of interracial relationships feel the way they do about the issue, but the key to their harbored feelings is that there are still huge relational differences between most Blacks and Whites in America.

Over time, many instruments that have been designed to brainwash and condition the minds of minority race members in order to propose the image of this mythical, supreme White being. This type of obstruction of truth encompasses America and is aided by the deceitful, misguiding hands of media, through the deceptive teaching of incorrect history and the unjust internment of innocent people. Because of the way America has adopted these iniquitous means of control for so long, the effects have been seen throughout all minority groups. The results are very unfortunate, most especially because they involve cases where the favoring of 'Whiteness' has turned certain Black men against their own people as well as themselves. From their own eyes, these types of men disconnect themselves from, and lose touch with the realities of the African American people. As a result, they are immediately labeled as 'Sellouts', and become ostracized from Black grace.

Conjointly, racism's past and present existence automatically tightens the boundaries of interracial dating statuses. When it comes to corporate America, Black men still struggle to reach certain levels of success and acceptance. They never really feel that they reach the same level of their White counterparts. History shows us how Blacks were purposely held out of high positions for so long that when some were finally allowed into those positions, they rushed in unprepared and misused the power they were given. Now, some men overcompensate by switching roles. They create new identities for themselves and deny who they really are in addition to where they came from. They feel the need to accept as much 'Whiteness' as they can in order to blend into their world.

These are usually the acts of men who quarrel with Black women to the point of no return and try to thrust themselves into White favor. They do not deal with their own anger in these situations; instead, they blame Black women for the problems that stand between their successes and failures. These men believe they need to change their own images in order to take heed to their so-called, 'level of acceptance,' which was supposedly handed to them by the majority race.

Right From Wrong

There are what I like to call both acceptable and unacceptable reasons why Black men and women date and marry outside of their race. Those two reasons motivate people to make conscious decisions about interracial dating that they know will impact themselves and their potential offspring. The acceptable reasons for interracial relationships revolve around true love's essence and colorblind nature. The spirit of this type of reasoning repudiates all biased hatred of interracial connections, because it's righteousness speaks truth into the heart of life's virtue. It means that a man and a woman, regardless of religion or color, can fall in love and be happy together. This love is a strength that many traditional relationships lose or never attain. Love, which never dies, cannot become poisoned or tainted by society's personal issues. Whether it is White, Black, East Indian, or Jewish, love conquers all.

To be fair, I sympathize with Black women who oppose interracial relationships. The only thing I disagree with though, is the placement and legitimacy of those reasons. When speaking with a woman who has disgruntled feelings, I'll usually ask, "Do you think a Black and White heterosexual couple can honestly fall in love without prejudice or preference?" That woman's response always lets me know how reasonable her thoughts are and how open she is to the topic.

My belief is that a mixed White and Black couple has to be much stronger than any other couple within the confines of ethnicity, racism, and prejudice in America. These couples have to deal with stares and glares along with the remarks and maltreatment thrown from both sides of the fence. Even their children suffer from identity crisis issues that force them to choose sides. I would just hope for the parents to make an effective effort to teach those precious children about the evil ways of this world.

From another perspective, the unacceptable reasons for entering interracial relationships involve a great deal of bias and predilection. The people who use these unacceptable means are labeled as disloyal traitors and phonies. They are the ones who simply will not involve themselves with the women of their own race. Ultimately, those men do not have problems with Black women. They have issues with being Black themselves, and subliminally blame and punish Black women for it.

The bottom line is this: every person has their own issue, but to dismiss the beautiful women of one's own race is to dismiss one's self. There is nothing more shameful than a self-deprecating, weak man. How could someone, after a few bad experiences, write off an entire gender of his own people? There seems to be a similar issue concerning women and men who accept lesbian and gay lifestyles. Do they choose such lifestyles because they haven't been able to find suitable mates of the opposite gender? Black women and men should not believe that stepping away from their natural urges toward those of their own race and opposite gender could bring them more love or security. They should have more patience and realize that there are good and bad people all over the world. My opinion is that those types of men don't deserve the honor of a respectable woman of any race.

The company of a good woman has always been a blessing from God. Black women shouldn't waste their emotions on worthless men; they are not worth the time. Don't be down on yourself Black princesses. Keep your aim set on that Up High Man. He is worthy of your love and is eagerly searching for you as well.

Which Do You Prefer?

The preference issue is a very controversial subject that lies along the same lines as knowing what is right and what is wrong. There are some who simply prefer to date people of other races. For example, DeNiro has married two Black women and has dated a significant number of others. O.J.'s visual preference for White women seems to be nothing less than obvious, and Whoopi openly dates White men. You have to wonder what the original influential factors were for these people to decide to date outside of their races. Did they give up on the women and men of their own races, are they simply attracted to people of other races, or does it not matter at all? Who knows, but the one thing that neither should do is believe that a person of another race would treat them better than someone of their own. That is utterly impossible to predict.

Some Black women say they initially became interested in their White spouses because they found it difficult to meet Black men on their social levels. This may be true for many Black women, especially highly professional Black women. They also believe that there is a shortage of Black men on the same income and status levels. My response to this is, "Whites have monopolized America's entire economical and financial monster for so long that the majority of successful men who are now viewed as professional are obviously White and grossly overshadow the number of Black professional men." At the same time, it should also not be difficult to see that there is now an abundantly growing number of successful Black men in all professions. Does that spell shortage? Nope!

I completely empathize with Black women who feel they cannot discover the location of professional Black men, but that does not mean that Black men are somewhere, sitting around on sabbatical. Women just need to be a little more realistic in their search.

Sometimes, women can be so selective, that their selection process turns into being picky, and being picky could be the main reason why some women say they cannot find good Black men. In those cases, I would ask women, "Did you become tired of waiting and give up on Black men because you found that waiting was difficult?" My next question would be, "How comfortable are you and your White mate, knowing that his position and placement was secondary to begin with?"

That situation would never be mine because I, personally, love myself too much to settle for something I wasn't shooting for in the first place. Not being number one may be acceptable for some, but second place will never be acceptable for me, unless I start allowing impatience and lack of faith to be my leading tools of self-guidance.

In support of unbiased White and Black relationships, I can assume that there are circumstances when interracial relationships endure. When both partners remain racially color blind, no matter what kind of negative energy they get from their own particular racial group, they can survive in a healthy relationship. I'd take my hat off to those people any day. It takes a strong couple to keep an honest relationship alive in the United States, so I know that honest and successful interracial relationships are difficult to keep up with. If two people just happen to fall in love and have no preference regarding race, that is pure and honest love, and I cannot be so selfish as to not appreciate the relationship between them. No matter what race, creed, or religion, love is a beautiful thing and should be cherished.

Eight

The 12 Most Popular Myths About Black Men

"Only simpletons believe everything they are told! The prudent carefully consider their steps."
Proverbs 14:15

There have been countless numbers of articles I have read along with several radio broadcasts I have listened to, that have exhibited the unjustified bad-mouthing and persecution of Black men. Needless to say, I hated every minute of it, but I do believe that some of these subjects were not totally mythical. My purpose though, is to attack the blanket generalizations of negativity that people make about Black men. This does nothing positive for the image of the Up High man, struggling daily to keep his name untarnished. Now that I have the opportunity to share my thoughts, I will respond to some of the ludicrous remarks I speak of.

1. All Black men cheat in relationships.

How can anyone rationally make the statement that, "All Black men cheat in relationships," and believe there is such thing as a good Black man? Whoever they are, they must not know the meaning of the word 'contradiction'. This is a ridiculous claim that suggests all Black men have some type of uncontrollable deficiency that forces them to be dishonest and deceitful, while in committed relationships. This stereotype is similar to the ways in which the majority race has blasted African Americans in the past, by saying things like, "Niggers can't fly planes, be quarterbacks, or invent anything." Does this sound familiar? They need not do this anymore, because we apparently have found a way to do it to ourselves. It must stop now.

2. There is a shortage of good, professional Black men.

This is yet another absurd statement made by misinformed people. I personally believe that the numbers have gotten better, especially for Black women, now that they have forced themselves into the eyes of the professional world. However, this does not mean the majority of Black men are not taking advantage of their opportunities.

Secondarily, when I think of a shortage, I think of something that is either out of stock or virtually impossible to find. That, however, is not the case with the majority of the African American male community.

Men: Those of you who are living righteously and honestly, I recognize and honor you. Many sisters know your situation and feel your pain. However, there are brothers who are having a lot of trouble making correct decisions in their lives. Those men need to get off of their butts and start taking active steps toward success. You can help them by leading by example and by supporting them.

Women: I know all of you are not unrealistic in your judgment of the state of Black men. Please continue to be strong. We all need you and your strength. We men have a lot of difficult, deep seeded issues that blind us from time to time, and would like things to change overall. Please help your sisters understand this and motivate them to have more faith in their thoughts and words. Thirdly, I believe that the definition if the word 'race' is obvious. Life for many ethnic groups is a race. Our American situation is and always has been a competition, and the opposition between races has consistently proven to serve as a constant reminder of the amount of disgust that others pin against the Afro-American standard of living. You see, the people who control mass media's broadcasts also control the information that is released to us and kept from us.

Those same people alter factual data and persuade others to believe that Blacks still only represent 12% of U.S. population, and that there were less then a million men at the Million Man March. Persuasion and manipulation is their art. One thing they have become successful in doing is having us compare ourselves to the entire White race as well as other races. This is exactly why some of us believe there is a shortage of professional Black men. Sure, the percentages appear to be less than favorable, but when have those levels ever reached that of White equivalency? Never, that's when. Reality shows how there are more White men than Black men in America, and since Whites basically own America, you will more than likely see fewer Blacks in the professional environment than Whites. So it would actually be silly to compare. Don't let the numbers fool you. There really is no shortage of successful Black men in the professional world. We definitely need to do a better job in an effort to employ and self-educate all of our brothers, but our workingmen are at an advantage. Another bright point is that there are still more and more positions opening to Black employment and more fields and industries that are being taken over and run by Blacks.

3. Once Black men reach success, they have a greater tendency to abandon Black women for White women.

This is a tough one. Like many other accusations pointed at the head of any Black man, I know that this topic has been true in many circumstances. However, I believe that this specific allegation is generally over exaggerated. The truth to this claim, which lies behind the purposes of men who actually take part in this type of tomfoolery is very sad. It represents the acceptance of the notion that being White or preferring 'Whiteness' is dominant to that of any other ethnicity, as well as having a purity that is greater than that of any other skin color. Even though the mass media onrush advertises that, "White is beautiful, and everything else is a step down," many Black people are doing well in the categories of appreciation and love for each other. However, we are far from being out of the woods.

4. Strong, successful Black women intimidate and challenge the strength of Black men.

Most professionally successful Black women carry the desire for committed relationships with men. The assumptions that Black men sometimes make about those women limit them to the belief that those women have less of a need for men, once achieving their professional goals. Assumptions like these are devices we have created that work against ourselves and keep us from success. It seems that there is some unspoken fear of success that is hidden deep within some of our being that was left over from Master's whip. This type of thinking needs to stop now.

Believe it, the most successful Black woman is defenseless when it comes to love. The truth is that the more successful a woman becomes, the more she wants a man with whom she can share her triumph. They may have all the material items that tickle their fancies, but generally, women are well aware that the love of a good Black man is like no other. Most of these women are aggressive in their professions and may be a little domineering, but they are generally more submissive about their personal relationships with men. Very rarely do they bring their work personalities home to the bedroom. It is sometimes difficult for men to know the difference and be strong enough to approach these women, because some men are not yet comfortable with assertive women contributing to our society in major ways. Nevertheless, there are men like me who welcome successful women into our lives with open arms. Personally, I am weak for strong women who want to love me, so keep working ladies and you will get yours.

5. Black men are afraid to commit.

There are people who want to be involved in committed relationships and there are people who do not. The problem here is that many women do not take the time to find out about a man's relationship goals when they first meet. The thing to remember is that after discovering the commitment goals of your prospective partner, you will have a better chance of deciding whether to go forward or not. Lying about that desire can lead to confusion and anger.

Several women make the mistake of being dishonest with men when they say, "I am not looking for a serious relationship right now," or "Whatever happens, happens." This usually occurs when the woman doesn't want to scare the man off. Ideally, the man thinks, "The woman is not interested in a relationship," and plans accordingly. Later, the woman who wanted a relationship all along, begins to think of the possibilities of commitment with the man who has no knowledge of her change of heart. Next, she bluntly informs him of her relationship interest, which totally catches the man off guard. This confuses the man and makes him feel like he has been tricked, because he eliminated the possibility of commitment after hearing what the woman said in the beginning. At this point, the average situation involving this type of miscommunication is awkward for both the man and the woman.

In situations like the one above, men often feel that women act sneaky by not communicating that they had been forming feelings for a different type of relationship, and women most commonly have the opinion that the man is running from, or is afraid of commitment. This is a very easy problem to fix, but it requires the usage of honesty and trust.

To decrease the likelihood of this happening to you, be up front, and do not assume. This should let people know what your goals are and are not.

Another delicate issue that often affects the likelihood of men entering relationships is early sex. Many women habitually overcompensate during the beginning of relationships by allowing intercourse to happen before both partners are mentally ready. They have been known to be overly generous to men before knowing if they are worthy. With this being the case, men who do not have commitment as a goal, generally become comfortable and complacent, instead of feeling the need to work toward love and commitment. They also become easily tempted to delay or misdirect relationship talks.

To improve the outcome of dealings like this, I have formed a solution to aid women in the process of getting to know a man's values of commitment. This solution may not work in every situation, but for people who value honesty, it is simple.

To be successful with their inquiry, women should find out what men want and what they are not interested in. Ask the man about his desires regarding commitment. Another way to get answers out of him is to ask him to describe his idea of the perfect relationship, whether it involves a girlfriend or a wife. If he is passionate about his answers and seems sincere, his responses are likely to be honest ones. In most cases, a man who values commitment has thought this idea over before. If he stumbles in his answer or replies stating how he hasn't thought about it, then he's probably not interested. Don't be afraid to challenge a man's values. If he wants commitment, he will let you know.

6. Black men don't know what they want in relationships.

Figuring out if you want to be in a relationship is a lot easier than choosing the components you want to be included in that relationship. Men and women often get lost in the confusion at times and just can't figure out which way to go. On the flipside, I know that I want a woman who is attractive, considerate, funny, health conscious, family oriented, spiritual, honest, fair, loving, and has good credit. Keep in mind that it is possible for someone to actually possess every one of these characteristics, but most times they will not be perfectly tuned to your liking. That is where patience comes in to play.

When most single people think about what they want in a relationship, they have a tendency to veer outside of reality a bit and dream of perfection. This type of thinking is very optimistic, but it can be dangerous at the same time. Since there is no such thing as a perfect relationship, creating perfect images of a fairy tale-like relationship can actually be the same as creating relationship suicide. Everyone who seeks positive relationships should have positive, but realistic values that they would like to experience during the life of the bond. This would keep them grounded and full of hope.

The Black men a particular woman may have encountered in her past may not have always known what they wanted to happen within the confines of a committed relationship, but there are plenty of Black men who do know of their own desires and want them to become reality.

There are plenty of ways to tell if a person knows what they want in a relationship, although, I think the best way to tell is to ask. I'll also give a little advice and say, "If you are with someone who says they want commitment, but don't know what they want from the relationship, they obviously haven't thought it through enough to be ready for partnership." Do not settle for this. If you want someone who is sure about what they want in a relationship, you would be wasting your time with one who lacks that assurance.

"African American men have always wanted relationships with their women to include and be led by love, respect, and understanding. Let's look at the situation honestly. Just by receiving comments from several Black women, it is clear that they are angry, especially with Black men. If they would stop with the anger and replace it with love, perhaps they would provide better chances for themselves. This brings me to my point. If you choose a trifling man, then that is what you will have," Says Michael of Detroit, MI.

7. Black men don't know how to communicate what they want effectively.

This is sometimes true, but it is not a case that is solely promoted by Black men. I am sure that there are some Black men who do not communicate well in relationships, but our communication as a people is a greater issue. If a woman wants effective communication with her man, she should not settle for anything less. In some situations, though, the ladies go a little too far.

Many women have told me how their men won't call them to check in when they think the men should. They call that, "Not communicating effectively." This may be true for them; however, it all depends on the nature of your relationship. In my case, after dating a woman for a week, one day I found myself getting cursed out because I didn't call her in between the time I left work to the time I arrived at home. Here is an example of the difference between someone who cares and someone who feels as though they just want to keep tabs on another person. I knew I didn't want to feel like I was checking in with my parole officer when the crime had never been committed. Needless to say, I had to let her go.

8. Black men feel the need to compete with their significant others.

A little fun competition can be healthy in a relationship, but if the relationship is a competitive one, an order of separation might be necessary. Abusive relationships usually begin with men who are very competitive and territorial, and no sane woman wants that. For example, in cases where the man doesn't want the woman making more money than him, that should be the woman's signal to leave. If she's comfortable with taking a pay cut, then fine, but I think men like this have personal issues that they need to sort out on their own. These men may be this way due to insecurity, tradition, or jealousy. I, personally, would brag if my woman made more money than me, not that that's hard to do though.

9. Black men are insecure, overly aggressive, and territorial in their relationships.

This claim seems more relevant than most others, but it is not really direct. I am assuming that this claim relates to men who feel as though they have to set unfair rules and standards for their women to follow. One could also make this statement about White men, Arab men, Chinese men, or men from any ethnic background. I can understand why this would be a problem in a realistic circumstance, but singling out Black men to be the sole culprit is wrong. I personally feel like people are human and they do what they want to do. If a person's spouse wants to cheat on them, they probably will at some point. A person should not have to create preventative methods in order to lower the chances of their partner doing something they would not like. If you ever feel like you need to resort to these types of antics, you probably should not be with that person anymore.

10. If women only learned more ways to pamper and nurse Black men, the love would work.

Come on people. We all know this would do more harm than good. A grown man who takes care of his responsibilities should not need to be pampered or stroked. If you think you are with a man who needs pampering, please get him some professional help. Black men should never be treated like babies; maybe consoled and caressed, during hard times, but never babied.

11. All men want is sex.

All men are not after women for sex, however, the truth is that there are a lot of men out there who view sex from women as a prize. All women should be aware of this and become wise about who they let into their bedrooms. I am not suggesting that women make every man go through a three month waiting period before they give him the home telephone number, but being strategic about getting to know the guy can bring great benefits. The correct strategy can let you know who to cut off very early in the dating game, and who to invest in. Strategy can also give anyone the ability to notice and match values, tendencies, and habits. Overall, it is a good tool to use for the judgment of a person's character.

12. A man must have a high paying job, fancy car, and be over six feet tall with no kids in order to truly be a good man.

Again, the most important thing we must realize with this myth is that a good Black man cannot be defined in the same way we define successful White men. America's tainted image of the acceptable levels of etiquette and propriety obviously does not include the Black man. Men who have their heads on straight know that success cannot be attained just by having money and cars, because they are aware that those material items hold no true value. They are also aware that the act of judging personalities by material possession is wrong.

The power that controls America's mainstream media organizations has already placed into the minds of American citizens, the ideal model for success and goodness amongst men, and most times, Black men are not a part of that display. Those models exude thoughts, which suggest how a Black man, who doesn't have the highest paying job or luxury car is not a good Black man. This does not sound fair, does it? Where is our focus, beloved? How do you think the men with lower incomes who work hard to support their families feel about this? What about our bus drivers, office workers, teachers, and salesmen? Can men with these careers not qualify as potential bachelors or good men? Why do they stand lesser chances of dating nice looking women who care? Once again, where is our focus?

Nine

The Position of Our Youth

Today's youth are tomorrow's champions. If we ignore the importance of their roles, we sabotage our legacy; but if we nurture their growth, we have only to receive honor in their success.

The issue of family influence has been a very controversial topic within the African American community for quite some time. Suffering from the overabundance of illegitimate households, the lack of positively projected role models, and the allowed mis-education of our history has made many of our young men struggle in their efforts to create and sustain realistic goals and positive conditions that would assist immensely in their achievement of righteousness, success, and accomplishment. These causes of which I speak, are currently eradicating the confidence levels and affecting the emotional dispositions of our future leaders. It is through this, that confusion has replaced fraternity and community on many levels, and continues to spiral downward. These are the facts.

While hunting for a justifiable cause, some may point fingers and say, "Young people are crazy these days," but my opinion is that the younger generation has definitely gotten a little help along the way from the earlier generations, which weren't necessarily the perfect examples to follow.

Causes for changes within the traditional confines of the actions of our youth carry an enormous variance, but to be specific, illegitimacy is one that stands out from the rest. I don't know when it happened, but it seems as though illegitimacy has somehow come to be accepted in our society. What happened? Is it no longer shameful to birth children into broken families without thoughts of matrimony? There were once strong, honorable lines discouraging premarital sex and fooling around. Being a lady was once the most prominent lesson for our young Black sisters, and it was equally unacceptable for men not to care for their families. Raising children in poverty also used to be an occurrence that rarely took place in our communities, but now our priorities have changed. What type of affect do you think this has on children being raised today?

One major note of light is that fatherless home lifestyles for African America have become prevalent, due to of the disregard for family union and the allowance of pregnancy outside of marriage. This is a problem that must be addressed in every household. Having babies with boyfriends should never challenge the act of having children within the boundaries of marriage. It just does not seem acceptable to me. To others, however, marriage may not be an option. In my opinion though, having a baby is not a phase. It is a privilege, therefore, not being responsible enough to protect oneself or their potential offspring clearly shows signs of self-destruction and confusion.

Systematically speaking, raising children in complete family environments serves as a model for success and should be the goal of every Black man and woman, as it is the healthiest environment to bring children up in. For example, the idea of women believing that they don't need men, and that they can do just as good of a job raising their kids by themselves is insane. Families are proven to be most triumphant when thriving in a complete status. The harmony created by such, provides an unspeakable opportunity to create happy memories and live most productively.

When fathers are not around, it can be very difficult for our male children to learn lessons thoroughly and in the time most beneficial for their growth. Issues like protecting themselves and providing for their own children and women sometimes come late or not at all, without the guidance of dads. Just imagine how handicapped the next generation will be if proper action is not taken now.

Many people advise how the use of male role models such as uncles, boyfriends, or mentors could help with the development of our young men, although, none of these positions could ever provide the same type of support and guidance that a father could.

On another note, change in tradition has very little to do with the change in the times, however, it has everything to do with our culture and how we celebrate and support it. If our fight for equality and civility hadn't died years ago, sure, things would be different, but is that the fault of our young people? I do not believe so. For it is through abandonment and outright neglect that forces our babies to grow up angry, afraid, and confused. Whether we mean to place them in these environments or not, it is the responsibility of the older generation to repair the damage inflicted. It is because of prior efforts, or the lack there of that paved the way up to now. So, instead acting like prophetic saints, we all must take on some responsibility in an effort to uplift our future and protect our interest by showing them love, whether it be tough or soft-hearted. The solution is not to ward them off, lock them away, or fight against our younger generation. It is through a greater connection that our promise land will be found.

In essence, nurturing, molding, educating, and protecting our children from themselves and others is the surest method of incorporating reparation. We must take this responsibility as our own. It is not up to our government, members of the Caucasian society, or mainstream television media to give us the understanding or tools we need, because we naturally obtain both. Don't forget that it was the trickery of our captors that made us believe that we were useless, with no capability at all. Since these myths are now dead in the water, our understanding and strength can now give us freedom, not from our captors, but from the hindrances of the effects from the past that we may now acknowledge.

In the chapter entitled *The Woman's Point of View*, I intimately express my concern toward issues pointing to the intended misdirection of truth, related to positive images of Black male role models in this country's description of Back males; especially as displayed within the nations main vehicle of information namely, television. Outside of that, the topic of mothers raising families says a lot about why many of our children grow up confused. Because so many African American fathers have been removed from their families, the result has left us with young boys looking wherever they can to find exemplary icons to emulate. Whether the model is a family member, abusive boyfriend, or rap star, our boys are learning from somewhere, and that is a fact. "What will help," you ask? Well, there are limitless amounts of answers to that question, but I will tell you that falsely informing our boys of an idea about how people feel good Black men are a dying breed, will not only hurt the ones expressing complaint, it will destroy the hope of our people and lower the chances and goals of our boys, who want to be the good men that most of us have lost hope for. Let us now create pathways of success for our young men instead of narrow roads leading toward dead ends.

Miseducation and Deculturization

Since the slave trade, the most powerful tool of African captors and oppressors has been miseducation. Existing as a term used to describe the disparaging effects on the global African American psyche, miseducation, which redirects truth and reality, has a historic reputation for being used as a force to twist the positions of the African people and culture.

The reality of this country being built from deep levels of deception and lies, grants Blacks the opportunity to either accept or reject the falsehoods forced into their minds as small children eager to learn. From completely distorted ideas about George Washington's sense of honesty, to Columbus' hidden truth of his murderous character, America was built from deceit and blood. In terms of deculturization, America's routinely effective process of manipulation through the monopolization of control has worked like a demonic charm. It has successfully been utilized to lobotomize many African Americans in an effort to force them to accept the culture and highly exaggerated supremacy of Europeanism.

For a very long time, public school systems all across America have been failing to provide adequate schooling for Black Americans, and in turn, are brainwashing mass amounts of the African American population. By teaching about fictitious occurrences and events, many manipulators, **sorry** I mean many teachers, wrongfully mislead students and take advantage of their eagerness to learn by providing half-truths and abounding lies about history. Existing as more than an accident, the plan of disconnecting African Americans from their culture and native soil has done everything to please all efforts of White domination.

The key here is that everyone who understands the power of education understands the necessity for it's being. This truth exposes the true intent of our oppressors and proves their long supported theory of White grace and reverence. It is very plain to see. Even traditional Christian proponents flaunt notions of European views by disregarding the effects of anti-African Americanism through their disregard of direct messages of destructive advertising delivered by the majority race's giant media monster, and by their utter neglect shown toward urban education issues and racial inequities.

Also, when it comes to defining self, the trained minds of many African Americans have forced the restriction of thought and contemplation into everyday living. Unfortunately, this has created a great subliminal disdain for change, sided by pessimistic feelings of inferiority. By thinking this way, many Blacks limit themselves to items of cultural and African reference, while turning to more of a European frame of sight. Being forced to live this way, African slaves became helpless in their effort to maintain their heritage and slowly began losing ties to it. This aspect of deculturization is the part that should be taught and studied, because of the necessity for its destruction.

On a whole, the mental incarceration that my people and I have fallen victim to shall be conquered and abolished forever. From studying the history of the world, one could see how all ancient dynasties came to an end, and could simultaneously assume how this one is on it's way out. However, first we must choose to expand our cultural frames of mind and consciously embrace our African and American heritages. When this happens, our mental incarceration will cease.

Closing the Gap

The first step in the battle against the alien mindset (Alien: *not contained in or deriving from the essential nature of something*) of African Americans is to properly instill the essential formula of truth, which will surely neutralize and dismantle all instruments of impediment built against our progression. We must create a task of concentration geared toward private education programs best fit for our needs and goals. Ultimately this type of adjustment will help in the production of resources that would benefit our collective societies and neighborhoods. This way, the reliance on our self-production, as opposed to the goods produced by other cultures, would be more of a popular approach.

We, together, must work endlessly to destroy the slavery mindset and all deeply rooted impressions forced onto us by our captors. We must continue to break their cycle and focus on our own. To do this, we have to make it redundantly clear that mental slavery is no longer an acceptable state of mind. It is crucially important that we stand to renounce manipulation, and accept the responsibility to change, not just our sense of existence, but theirs as well.

Ten

We Need Each Other

Issues Close To Home

Someone was hurt before you; Wronged before you;
Hungry before you; Frightened before you;
Beaten before you; Humiliated before you;
Raped before you; Yet, someone survived!

Maya Angelou

Despite our issues and concerns with each other, we Black men and women must realize that we need each other to survive. Our problem of disconnection continues to exist because our women and men are confused and wrong about a lot of things. In many cases, men don't know what women really want from them, and women remain frustrated and tired, as they assume the worst; which echoes thoughts that good Black men are on the brink of extinction. Overall, some of our ways of thinking have become misguided, but are not totally off track.

Throughout the history of the world, there have been many civilizations and races that have vanished from the earth's surface. Several of those races once struggled for their own survival and lost the fight. You may not see it so clearly, but we too are struggling for the core of our existence. The way I see it, we need to have our own interests in mind, but it is difficult to focus on those interests because we are too busy hating and killing each other. One thing I have come to understand is that the relational reconnection of our men and women may not happen during our lifetime, but the hint of reality's coldness shows that if our men and women's disdain for one another continues to grow, and if we continue to ignore the importance of raising our children correctly, our race will certainly die.

Of the many purposes for the delivery of this book, the main one has always been to help empower African American relationships with the hopes of increasing the rate of marriage within our communities. I remember fantasizing about married life as a child and still feel that marriage and companionship are important goals for men, women, and children. Other ethnic groups rush to advertise percentages and statistics of the decline in Black marriages and have no concept of its cause. In response, I feel that it is quite difficult and utterly impossible to have a complete understanding of the positive and negative aspects of Black marriages, without having knowledge of the iniquitous historical factors that have contributed to the physical and mental separation of the union. These factors have placed an unequivocally severe strain on the marital and premarital relationship goals of heterosexual African Americans, which has also added to the precipitous decline of marriages in our communities.

It is a proven fact that the tides of marriage have changed dramatically within our lifetime. According to the 1960 U.S. Census Bureau, African American homes held a marriage rate between 78%-80%, while dropping to an astounding 16% in 2000. On top of those statistics, the number of Black married couples is only half that of White married couples. Looking a little deeper will help you see the number of unmarried adult men and women is increasing, while floating a little above 40%. Also, knowing that there is a greater population of Black women than men makes that 40% sting a bit more. Those are their statistics. Let's move on.

Marriage was created as the sole institution through God, for the union of man and woman. Two of the reasons for the creation of this matrimonial alliance were companionship and procreation. These words are very important because they point to the heart of our very existence. If you look back at those reasons and think, you will realize that both, not one, are necessary for our survival. That means if there were a problem with one of those important factors, then we would be in big trouble. Now, we all know that we Blacks do not have a problem with child production, but we have become very weak in the companionship category. This is not acceptable, because the natural order behind raising children includes figures of the male and female gender. This unfortunate realization forces me to inform you that we have a major crisis on our hands. Our very existence is in grave danger. In actuality, we are currently confronted with one of the biggest crises in the history of the African American people, and we must defeat it.

The number one cause for divorce in America is money. Equally important, unemployment has slowly and dramatically decreased the lot of marriage-worthy Black men. With that being true, we can also throw the AIDS epidemic, drugs, alcohol, homosexuality, thug life, and victims of violence into the pot of reasons why the institution of marriage for African Americans has declined. However, the contention not yet mentioned is that the number of good Black men has also increased. Nobody wants to see that except those not tainted by the poisonous media. The truth is that we are suffering, but we are also on the rise.

There are still many Black folk creating vehicles of empowerment so we may once again travel the Underground Railroad to righteousness. We must succeed at this because it is imperative that we repair our union. The only difference is, this time, the railroad will be above ground.

We must grasp the opportunity to mend our relationships as Black men and women, so our children can learn the correct ways of interaction with one another. By recreating a positive and inspiringly determined love for each other, we can set the path for our own future. Who else has that opportunity?

Slavery's Stinging Remnants

Although slavery wasn't the only reason for the destruction of Black marriage and family life, it was the catalyst for the sabotage of it. Even though this is the truth, we cannot continue focusing our attention on bashing the majority race for their part in slavery and its outcome, as we do. We need to concentrate our attention on what we can do to construct a better place in America together.

One thing that is often swept under the rug is that we are suffering by way of America's hypocritically incorrect, racist system that unjustly penalizes Black boys and girls for no reason at all. Secondarily, too many Black community institutions have been destroyed and weakened by the growing rate of incarcerated Black men. The solution of those in power is to build more jails, as opposed to improving our educational system. It is very clear that the powers that be are expecting Black men to go to jail and are aiding that process. That has always been America's problematic way of handling things; hide it, lock it up, and forget about it. That is why there have been so many questionable circumstances in American history, and there is still so much of it we will never know about, because of the deceitful minds of our so-called American leaders.

The selling of slaves largely contributed to the separation of families and the severance of relationships. Many politicians once forbade African American marriage and punished those who did not take heed. Their hate promoted even worse negativity than the today's present display toward gay marriage. They did this to keep Blacks separate and to project incorrect ideas about them. Black males were ultimately perceived as being dishonest, sexually driven beasts, incapable of the committed institution of marriage. Another perception about Black men still lingering, is that they are aggressive and totally out of control. This did exactly the same thing it does now. It makes people fear the Black man, want to lock him away, and treat him like an animal.

Also, research has provided me with the insight that the fathers of Black families were often made out to be deserters and were viewed as being insensitive to the needs of their people. There were many historical claims written by whites that have suggested that even the mothers of families denied the father's role in the production and progression of the family. Again, these are negative images supplied by the aggressors for one purpose. That purpose was to disempower the Black race and never let it rise. This remains consistent with this country's continuing tendency to neglect and discount the male within families of African America. Their plan was to create the best magic trick of all time, which was to make the Black man disappear without putting him on a boat. The interesting thing about this is that it has worked to some degree. It is now time to unravel that plan.

Fatherless Homes

I am what I like to call a successful product of a single parent home, thanks to my mother. I have grown into a successful, independent man who will one day value a happy marriage, family, and home. Although I claim success, I didn't cross the finish line without bruises. I believe that having a good father around to teach and mold me could have helped me avoid the majority of those bumps and could have helped decrease the amount of the bruises. This makes me wonder about other people's thoughts and beliefs of their own success with and without their fathers. One question I have asked has been, "Are children as likely to become successful in fatherless, single parent homes as they would be in homes with their fathers present?" Looking at both sides of the spectrum, I can honestly answer no to this question and proceed to explain how dual, heterosexual parented homes would especially fill in a lot of the wide gaps for young African American boys.

There are countless amounts of successful Black men who grew up without fathers and that success is a wonderful thing. Many of these same men, however, while looking back at their own experiences, stated that their father's absence did not affect their level of success either way. That basically meant, having a father would not have helped add to their success. These guys couldn't have been more mistaken. How can one say that growing up with a loving, supportive father may or may not do anything positive for their success? It almost sounds like these people are saying they'd be better off without a father, or it wouldn't matter either way. They would not dare say that about their mother though. They'll quickly tell a friend or associate, "I don't know what I would do without you," but when it comes to real dads, they apparently become expendable at a minor loss. How is that? It is my opinion that not having a father around could be as detrimental and devastating as not having a mother in one's life. They are both the most nurturing and totally necessary components involved in the lives and growth of children and young adults. How could an honest person, not speaking solely out of emotion, deny that?

Many studies have shown that the lack of fathers, not race, is by far the most accurate determination of whether or not a child will end up in poverty or in prison. Today, 60% to 70% of Black children are born into fatherless homes. 70% of long-term prison inmates and 70% of juveniles in reform institutions were raised without a father. 87% of all Black children living in poverty are raised in single-parent homes. Could they have had more successes in their lives if their fathers gave a damn? Of course they could have.

Reading this information should give you an idea of how important family is. We, as men, need to introspect and face our issues. Why are we running away from our responsibilities and future? Our women are suffering and we have to save them from bearing the weight alone. My message to those women who suffer reflects that of deceased rapper Tupac Shakur when he said it best in his hit song *Keep Your Head Up.* Because of God's grace for his children, things will become easier and things will get brighter, but in order for those things to happen, we must come together and strengthen our levels of unconditional love toward one another.

Women Who Keep Their Children From Their Fathers

When I was a boy, my father had already begun his life as a drug abuser and a criminal. As I got older, I started asking my mother about him and why he was not around. She always gave me the truth, even though my curiosity drifted. She knew my father had broken both of our hearts several times over, yet she never spoke poorly of him to me, nor did she deter me from having a relationship with him. Since becoming a man, I have realized how much I respect my mother for being so strong and fair. I understand the simple fact that she gave me the chance to learn, on my own, who my father was. She also gave him a chance to learn who I was and who I wanted to be.

Presently, my father and I speak occasionally, but not enough. Even though we have both tried, I can only admit that things will be the way they are until he either decides to change his ways or until we both improve our communication efforts. Ether way, I do see light at the end of the tunnel.

My mother who never lied to me about my father, made sure I knew my paternal family members intimately and taught me a life lesson about fairness and equality. Because of that, I am able to forgive and respect.

By now, I'm sure you can understand my situation, and I am positive that you can better assume the likely situations of other people who are or were products of single parent homes, headed by Moms. I'm also sure that you, being an honest, opinionated reader, can give me an honest answer to the question that I am about to ask. Do you believe that a child raised in a single parent home, headed by his or her mother, would be better off if the father was also in the household? Although this may seem like a no-brainer, many people respond by stating how it probably wouldn't make a difference; however, I beg to differ. No offense to those who respond this way, but I don't think you are doing the math correctly. Families, naturally and traditionally include mommies, daddies, and kiddies, if the birds and the bees are in flight of course. Therefore, don't you feel that going against the grain would bring some form of turmoil?

Getting back to the issue at hand; I would like to oppose and give a good old fashioned, "Shame on you," to all women who refuse visiting rights or any type of communicative interaction between their children and their children's fathers, especially if the fathers are actually trying to be good dads. Break-ups occur and divorces happen. That is one part of life we either get hung up on or move past. Here is a straight forward question for you: "In relationships between men and women, who creates the problems, or decides to separate? The answer is both participants, right? The man and, or the woman. Okay, here is a better question, in case you didn't get that one. Why do so many women make their children suffer because they can't get along with their partners? I ask these questions because these situations do actually occur, and they happen more than you know.

Bitter mothers, angry because the relationship didn't work out, sometimes find ways to hurt the dads by keeping thier kids from them. Sure, they try to justify their actions by giving some off the wall reason about how the child's father isn't a good person, or how him having another woman just won't do, but the reality is always that those women's issues lie with the men, not the kids.

Women, please take a deeper look and think about things fairly. If you act in a way that is similar to this, you must understand that you are not just punishing your ex-lover, you are punishing and scarring your children and their futures. Fathers are needed, and no matter what grave mistake you thought he made in the past, outside of dangerous behavior, children need and deserve to be exposed to their fathers.

On a personal note, I would like those same women to know that I do not judge or look down on them for what they do or have done. If you are reading this right now sister, I want you to know that you can change things. Your heart does not have to be cold. Your children can grow up and thank you for allowing them to see that you made the right choices, whether their relationships with their fathers were successful or not. We cannot live life if we hold onto grudges and pass blame as much as some of us do. Give your children a chance to see things for themselves, so they can make their own decisions.

I am often overwhelmed with complete admiration when I am out and see dads spending time with their children or pushing them in strollers. Actions like these exemplify who I would like to become someday. I think of great dads as heroes and that is how I want someone to think of me some day. Men, our children are precious and they are depending on you, as am I.

Men Who Take Care Of Their Children

Some women say they don't need or want men to help raise their children because of the feeling that they can do everything by themselves. They tend to believe that there would be no difference in the lifestyles of their children if there were a man in the house. Their claim also extends a very demeaning message by stating, "Most Black men don't take care of their own kids." My thoughts about this force me to, yet again, immediately dismiss and battle all mass generalized statements causing harm to magnitudes of Black men, not only taking care of their kids, but caring for children produced by other men with whom the mother had ties to. Do they get their credit? How much do we hear about the loyal men who bust their behinds to put food on tables for their families? Even worse, do you tell that good man who takes care of his family, you appreciate him for being there, while setting the right example?

Let me explain something. It is true that many of our good, wholesome women are abused, mistreated, and under-appreciated by men, who don't deserve them. On behalf of the weakness of those men, I sincerely apologize, knowing I can never repair the damage done. Please forgive me, and the rest of my brothers, ladies. The pain that our Black sisters and mothers feel and endure is real and cannot be downplayed, but the actions stemming from the emotions abroad can be controlled.

As human's, we are very fragile creatures with an abundance of uncontrollable emotions; the most dangerous being anger. Through anger, we sometimes create situations that don't produce positive results. One of many examples points to how people, especially children, feel when they believe they have been stepped over or looked past. Abandonment is the first thought that comes to mind, which usually brings on withdrawal and depression. This causes people to feel that the best way to protect themselves is to put up a wall by saying, "I don't need you." This result often creates pain that not only reaches the necessary target, but it also hits innocent men and fathers, living righteously. No woman alive who truly values a good man can ever honestly say she has no need for a good man, because with him, her desire lies.

To decrease the destructive onslaught of the image of our good, paternal population, we should stop acting as though we don't really need our good dads. Bad guys come a dime a dozen and deceive more women every day, but there are also plenty of our African American fathers who are not hard to find and who are not extinct, so let's not treat them that way.

Baby's Momma

Singers sing about it, and rappers rap it in their rhymes. My question is, "What in the world is a baby's momma?" As I understand, this term has evolved from a reference into a label. Maybe it's my ignorance that keeps me from understanding this expression's relevance, and maybe that same unawareness leads me to believe that society's view on *baby's mommas* does nothing but serve as a mockery of single mothers who value companionship with men. From my perspective, some women use this term as a way of expressing, "I am not married, but I do have a child by a man who I am not with." The image I see is a woman who has two or three kids, each by different men, and has wed none of them. In most cases, the pregnancy was an alleged accident. Message! Time Out... I want to make this clear to the people who simply do not know. Pregnancy is never an accident. The penis and vagina are tools for reproduction. Since this is a known fact, we should also be aware that pregnancy occurs after the penis is inserted into the vagina; then fertilization occurs. Therefore, unless a penis somehow trips itself up, falls inside a vagina, and stays there long enough to ejaculate, pregnancy can never be an accident. No matter what anyone says or thinks, if you have sex, you are taking steps to make a baby. There is not one contraceptive device in the world that is 100% pregnancy proof. The only true way to avoid pregnancy is to not have sex at all. Abstinence can help in more ways than one. In my case, abstaining from sex for an entire year taught me a lot about myself. It showed me that I had a great amount of discipline. It also taught me a lot about how people let lust affect their choices and decisions, and that I had the power to refuse lustful lifestyles. You may want to give it a try. You might learn some important things about yourself and your spirit.

In my mind, the correct way to define the term 'baby's momma' is to say "The mother of a child." So, the question I have is why can't a happily married mother be recognized as a baby's momma? Most answer, "Because that doesn't sound right," but that's really what she is, right? Somehow, someone has taken the term and made it into a title with a status. The street definition of this term is "*The mother of children, with whom the father did not marry and is not currently involved.*" My opinion is that no one would even want to marry her because of the way she accepts the controversial label. An example of this is, "She ain't nobody, she's just my baby's momma." Since this is the case, I wonder how this label could be used as a way to promote single mothers, working hard for their families. Where does this negative connotation come from and why are so many women proud about referring to themselves as a *street defined* baby's momma? This is no way for us to relate to our mothers. Some of you may disagree or think that I am over-analyzing the issue but before you do, ask yourself, "Would I want my daughter to be a baby's momma one day?" I doubt the answer will be yes.

I understand that the accepted icons of single parenthood are the women who have a great deal of strength and raise children successfully on their own. That strength is what should be celebrated, not the idea of single parenthood. That is what I feel is happening in many cases. More and more women are having babies because of what they call accidents. "I'm a baby's momma and that makes me a strong Black woman," some say. These women are confused about a few things. To be able to take that title and make it your own, you must first become responsible and wise enough to make good decisions that reflect your intentions. Saying you are strong because you are a baby's momma is not one of them. Saying you are strong because you are a good parent is. I fully support single women who are raising their children well, while struggling without husbands or partners. Please continue to be strong. We need you more than ever.

Can't We Just Get Along

Anger has become very problematic in our society but does it have to be? Can we change the way we become upset or the way we handle disagreeing with each other, without being disrespectful to the ones dearest to our hearts? Sounds good, right? Why not give it a try? It would benefit you to give it a shot, but your partner has to be willing as well. Teamwork is a very important factor here.

On another note, I absolutely hate going back and forth about the same issues over and over again. We all know how things went down. Can we please eliminate or at least minimize the redundant interpretations of the sequence of events? This kills during arguments.

Learning to submit is another good strategy that quells the heated elements of the most vicious arguments. Simply apologizing for something, even if you didn't mean to hurt the other person's feelings does great wonders.

If you really want to exude strength, practice the art of submission. When I say submit, I don't mean beg like a dog, but put your ego away long enough to allow yourself to give in, and yield to your partner. That, my friends, takes strength. Submission actually strengthens relationships by diminishing negative pride and by birthing senses of vulnerability and humility. It's all about taking the time to put your pride down long enough to say you didn't mean it, and make up. It is amazing how some people won't even do that, but in the next sentence will be swearing up and down about their unconditional love for that person. Remember, consideration is the key. If you refuse to be considerate, you may reap what you sow in the end.

Some women become guarded when they hear the word 'submit', but that's only because their familiarity with the term usually carries hints of abuse and manipulation. Men, don't let that fool you. Women want you to captivate them and make them yours, in a good way of course. Be smart, but remain aggressive. The Bible states that a woman should submit to her husband and I believe that, just as I believe a man should do the same. There is equality in its very being. How the word has been translated and manipulated, however, has brought great confusion and concern. Never fear though; I have corrected the myth and have set things straight.

Insecurity

Why is it that women bend over backwards for manipulative men who lie and cheat on them, but as soon as a good man comes along, their walls go up? What is your opinion of this? It seems to me that feelings of insecurity along with decreased comfort levels, play big roles in the trade off.

Insecurity sometimes causes women to assume certain things, out of uncertainty. They sometimes do this so much that their assumptions ultimately replace questions, optimistic thoughts, and productive communication. This way of judging destroys chances for honesty and trust, and drives people away, causing big problems for that good man when he arrives.

Sometimes you will come across, or hear about a man who cares and wants to help this type of woman through her issues. Other times, you will come in contact with men who are not interested in fixing the mindsets of women. Neither type of man is wrong, but they both suffer equally, as does the woman.

Men want to be trusted as do women, but the walls have to come down and must be brought down for the right people. "Who is the right person," you ask? Well, you have to figure that out on your own, but know that starting out with the wall being up is not always the best strategy. For women, a great way to begin is to learn to master your skills of perception and sift through the roughage of men in the world. You should always start with you and your issues first, and worry about others later. If you enter a relationship as a dysfunctional mess, then that good man will probably notice that mess. Hone in on your plan of noticing good men, ladies, and you will see improvement in your selection.

Trust, Love, and Friendship

How is it that it is so easy to love, but not trust or be friends? My problem may be that I focus on the meanings of words too much. This forces me to think about statements and words as their definitions describe them. In situations like these, I wonder how someone could have a friend and not trust them. I also speculate on how a person could love someone and not trust them or be a friend to them. It sounds mystifying doesn't it?

In the past, I have been involved with women who have expressed love for me, but knew they didn't trust me. In addition to that, the friendship in those relationships was very weak. To this day, I still wonder how they thought they loved me, because a person cannot love truly without trust.

There are plenty of additional examples in my dating experiences where I was faced with uphill battles that left me fending for my honor and word. I had never before witnessed such a lack of trust and space from women. When it came to phone issues, not only did they not like it when I answered mine, they also hated when I did not answer, and even when it rang. I became so confused at one point, that I considered getting rid of the phone all together. Then I snapped out of it and realized that whether I answered the phone or not, I was not the one with the problem. It was the insecurity of those women that forced them to have their opinions. They did not trust me and there was nothing I could do about it. Since then, I have decided to be patient with women and compromise when need be, but I will never again fall for the mental abuse I was victim to. At one point, I felt guilty and almost believed I had cheated, when I had not; but no more. I chose to start things in a different way. "When meeting women," I thought, "I should communicate a little better, in terms of who Aaron Smith is."

Right then, I chose to make a change in myself that would possibly help the women I dealt with in the future.

Now, I begin by letting women know who I am, how I operate, and what I would like to happen in my next dating or long term situation. I put everything out in the open and tell them that I will answer my phone if the call looks important and will excuse myself every time. If it does not seem important, it will not get answered. I understand that some sisters will accept and respect my method because of its honesty, and I equally accept the fact that others will choose to go elsewhere because of their trust apprehensions. Either way, I figure I am being honest in an attempt to build trust.

The Strong Black Woman

First and foremost, Black women have come a long way in our society and have busted down walls that both men and society have placed in front of them. It has been an admirable thing to watch those walls come down, however, in many cases there has been a bit of baggage that has come along for the ride.

The African American woman has gone through an inconceivable amount of pain and torture throughout her history. Given the long periods of degradation, rape, and slavery, all of which she has had to bear on her back, the Black woman should actually be extinct right now. Her resiliency, which comes from God's blessing, has revitalized her strength time after time. She has consistently risen form the ashes like the mythical bird, Phoenix. The Black woman has not just survived, she has succeeded and surpassed all obstacles in her path. Nonetheless, in spite of the Black woman's many triumphs, due to centuries of purposely-negative programming, she still needs to be reminded of her greatness. Unfortunately, Mother's Day, alone, will not do that job, television fails, and today's Hip Hop generation obviously refuses. Who knows, maybe we can organize a march or gathering to display our appreciation for the Black woman. I'm not just talking about men showing that appreciation. I'm saying everyone. Men, women, and children, together, should be a part of this act of paying homage to our mothers. If other ethnic groups wanted to join in, that would be great, but I am referring to a global sign of appreciation within the African American family. She should be glorified for her determination and strength. She needs to know that we all love her. She is our mother, sister, lover, daughter, and best friend. Our unconditional love for her cannot allow her suffering to persist.

The title 'Strong Black Woman' is a very important one. It describes the integrity and character of righteousness along with the everlasting amount of faith within this woman's very being. Her well-deserved name should never be thrown around or used in vane, but that is what's happening in a lot of circumstances. In the names of my praiseworthy mothers, I rebuke the mindsets of women who allow the mockery of her preciously attained level, and pray that they will one day strive for that same excellence.

Michael Baisden, an author and controversial radio personality, once had an interesting forum on one of his broadcasts. One of the questions he quizzed listeners with was, "What makes sisters strong Black women?" Before you answer this question on your own, think about it for a few seconds... Are you finished thinking? I hope you thought of some insightful answers, because most of the women who answered on the radio answered incorrectly. The point of the question was to expose the ideas of the types of women, confused about the title's meaning. It showed how the label, 'Strong Black Woman' is automatically adopted and passed around more than it is earned or deserved. Most women answered the question loud and incorrectly, and were silenced when they were corrected. Most responded, "What makes me a strong Black woman is the fact that I bought my own car, pay my own bills, own my own home, and don't need a man." WRONG!!! That sounds more like an independent woman standing on the threshold of hypocrisy. Some people just want to lay around on their butts dwelling in their own hypocritical limbo, shouting, "I'm a strong Black woman," while thinking someone is going to stand there shaking in their boots.

Here is the correction. Being strong has nothing to do with how much money you make, or what you do with it. It has very little to do with how eager you are to let people know that you don't need a man for anything. It has everything to do with your character, your value for personal enhancement, and your determination for success in every aspect of your positive desires. The strong Black woman does not try to look big and bad by saying, "I don't need a man for nothing," She knows better than that. I am not suggesting that the strong Black woman needs a man to complete her personality or financial gaps, but I am saying, she needs and wants a man to complete her by providing the quality necessities a good man can provide for her to feel naturally complete. She lets him know that she needs him regardless of how much money she makes or how many college degrees she has. She also shows a willingness to submit to her man and yield to the leadership of that man. This says nothing about obedience, domination, or restraint, but instead points to the idea of trust and the true role of a man. There is no need for the strong woman to go around shouting about who she is, because she knows who she is and it shows. She also knows she wants to love and marry a good Black man who loves her, and she will do everything possible to get to that point.

The strong man knows that a strong woman does not take away from his glory. Even if she has a good job and is financially successful, the man knows she has reached that level because of her strength and determination. Because of this, the strong man also knows that the tools the strong woman possesses give him the inspiration he needs to achieve his goals as well.

The Strong Black Woman's Relationship Goals

Before entering a committed relationship, the strong woman prepares herself by asking for God's wisdom and by making sure that the expectations she has for men are aligned with God's word. She works on her issues of concern and maximizes her time by strengthening her values. Within the relationship, she uses the patience she mastered to minimize yelling and screaming during debates and arguments. Because of that, she will be able to communicate effectively with her man while remaining calm. She also has reinforced her values of consideration, honesty, and loyalty. Keep in mind that none of these values are easily attained, but because of her determination and willingness to succeed, it becomes her joy to sacrifice for the greater good.

Native Bostonian Roxane, explained it best by stating, "It takes a lot to be a strong Black woman today, but we are blessed to have the strong influences of our mothers and grandmothers before us who have been able to survive in the most dangerous waters. You have no choice but to be strong for yourself, have strength for your Black man who is up against the world, and for the children you strive to make a better life for."

Guidelines For Strong Black Women

• You should first and foremost, create and maintain a fortified connection with God. You must have faith and accept the plan that God has for you, and love yourself with all of your heart.

• Hold your head high and take pride in your successes and your failures, because you know that both make you stronger.

• Be sincerely happy and supportive of others by encouraging and inspiring them to achieve their goals.

• You should understand that no one is perfect, including you. Be humble and step into the shoes of the other person sometime.

• Set high goals for yourself and never stop trying to become a better person.

• Have an undying dedication to the loved ones in your life and make necessary sacrifices for the betterment of your family.

• Realize that there is no 'I' in 'team'. The air of independence and individuality that you carry is great and cannot be recreated, but please don't let those characteristics cloud your judgment by allowing them to lead you to a place that hinders your vision of togetherness and unity.

• You absolutely must be able to put your pride aside and apologize for things, even when you think you may not be in the wrong. Just because you don't think you hurt someone doesn't mean you didn't. This is probably the hardest principle, but it takes a lot of time and unwanted emotion out of unnecessary arguments.

• Let go of your stubbornness, pride, and selfishness enough to be able to submit to your lover when you need to. This can quell a lot of unnecessary, ongoing feuds between the two of you. Some women challenge men to stand up to them and do not back down.

This can be a very dangerous way to interact with men because of the threat of violence. We Blacks have been fighting for hundreds of years. The last thing we should do is fight each other in our own bedrooms.

The Intimidation Factor

I call it a myth in many cases, but many men feel intimidated when faced with a woman who is more successful than they feel they are themselves. In most cases this is not necessarily the fault of the woman, because she strives to succeed and break down barriers built against her everyday. However, I do place some degree of fault into the hands of the women who think their jobs, houses, and cars are what give them strength. I do this because it takes away from the true meaning of what *strength* represents. Their distorted view of strength, being fed by monetary and material possessions, creates a facade, which makes those women believe that a man who does not have those material possessions is not strong and remains unworthy. This is the trick we play on ourselves. What this does is create yet another path of separation between Black men and women. It also makes the man who doesn't have those items feel as though he is not complete, and that he must have these things in order to be able to win the successful Black woman. As a result, there are many men who are left with issues of insecurity. Therefore, out of the fear of having nothing to offer, men may not want to be with women who make more money than they do. This type of man is afraid that women will look down on him and leave him for a man with more wealth. It's funny how the mind works isn't it? This is another form of unnoticeable discrimination that we use against ourselves. Again, I place blame onto the women who exclusively claim self-reliance and exclaim how they don't need or want a man for anything. This intimidates many men, especially the ones who fear rejection. Combined or separate, the fear of rejection and the fear of having nothing to offer, make many men question their success with successful women. As a result, they retreat.

Even though I provide these realistic circumstances, I make no excuses for brothers who should have more confidence. They should improve themselves so they may become invulnerable and appreciative to the idea of being with a woman who makes more money than they do.

The Keys To A Successfully Fruitful Relationship

Throughout all of the bad relationships and hard breakups, women are in pain and have difficulty letting that pain go. It is their right to be angry and upset about our situation as Black men and women, as it is the right of men as well.

Realistic people who are interested in honest relationships stand by key relational values such as communication, consideration, and honesty. Those people know that if one of those values is missing, no good will come out of it. How do you feel about this? Do you feel that we really do a good job in communicating effectively with one another? Do you think we are considerate enough toward each other? How about honesty?

When it comes to communication, which usually requires more listening than speaking, we have to be real with ourselves. There is not one type of natural relationship with another human that will survive without proper communication. The amount or level of communication that may be required for that particular relationship may vary, but it still must exist. Remember, there can never be unity without communication

Consideration is a very good tool that mainly adds to the longevity of relationships, as opposed to communication and honesty, which are required throughout. This value involves the process of standing in the shoes of the other person often times, so the most fair and equal viewpoints may be acknowledged. Consideration requires a fair amount of compromise and understanding, which are both excellent vehicles for sustenance.

Honesty speaks for itself. Nothing lasts without trust. There is no trust without honesty, and we need trust for everything. Trust also ties into faith a little, but stands as its own entity. It is such a strong virtue that it will affect every aspect of your life if you allow it to.

I hope you see the significance of these keys. If you are willing to sacrifice more, try incorporating each of them into your personality and not just your relationship. This will, in turn, help you become a better person, and not just a better lover. Remember that these are only the keys to successful relationships. That means they unlock the door; they do not open it. That has to be accomplished by the people in the relationship.

To end this chapter, I would like to share a piece of my heart and mind that I pray will spread into yours.

I HAVE A DREAM

I have a dream. I have a dream that, one day, we, as men and women will once again love and protect one another. I dream that all African Americans will take into full consideration, each of our individual emotions, beliefs, and values. Good folks, I don't know if you see it yet, but I am telling you that we have a major crisis on our hands right now. We have dropped from mountaintop to valley low, but those mountaintops that once rose so high will again, peak at the crest of the never-ending sky. We will once again standup for our rights and together, walk proudly to the beat of that African drum. Brothers and Sisters, I have a dream that you will love me and I will love you, no matter what the next person will say or do. We owe it to ourselves to fight for unity. I may not get there with you, but I want you to know that we are the chosen people now and our father, full of grace, did not bring us this far to be disgraced. So, Ladies, Gentlemen, Christians, Muslims, Atheists, Racists, Warriors, Thugs, Pimps, Players, Zulus, Kings, Queens, Saints, Popes, Presidents, Rappers, Musicians, Fornicators, Prosecutors, Back-stabbers, Uncle Toms, Strippers, Have-Beens, Authors, Poets, Police, Artists, Ambassadors, Senators, Mayors, Supervisors, Janitors, Reverends, Pastors, Bishops, Panthers, Crypts, Bloods, and Prostitutes, it is destined that we join in unity. We collectively, will dispel these illusions of hatred we present toward one another and shall once again walk side by side, and the glory of the Lord shall be revealed as all flesh watch together. This is our destiny. This is the faith I point you to, just as Dr. Martin Luther King Jr. did for us years ago. This is my dream and I just wanted you to know.

Eleven

Let's Stay Together

Communicating During Arguments and Disagreements

"The strong is not the one who overcomes the people by his strength, but the strong is the one who controls himself while in anger."

The Prophet Muhammad

The concern over the well being of the union of African American men and women remains paramount, however, the necessity for connective relation between the two currently remains to be one of the most controversial subjects among Blacks. Furthermore, because of the bitterness and pessimism that our women and men carry, many hopes of reconnection have greatly diminished.

When referring to companionship, it is imperative that we all understand the fact that there is no such thing as a perfect relationship. Because of that, there will always be obstacles that we will not be able to avoid. However, what two people do after confronting those obstacles will always display the character and maturity of their union. That information could help approximate the longevity of the relationship in addition to the amount of happiness within.

In previous chapters I focused on anger, pride, and submission, all holding delicate relevance that should always be safeguarded; so forgive me if I repeat myself. In light of the damage that these issues can cause, the efforts of communication, on behalf of both relationship partners is very important.

Capable of being controlled, anger sometimes slips past our defenses and appears at the most unpredictable and inopportune times. It is an emotion that can be noticed but difficult to eliminate once brought about.

When upset with their mates, some allow anger's persuasion to compel them into welcoming an uncontrollable state of negativity, which makes them feel that yelling and being nasty is the best way of communicating their displeasure. In addition to this thought, images of bickering Black couples has taken over popular views and has become the ill-famed model of how our men and women, "Must act." Falsely so, this idea has seized so many of our minds that a terribly gross generalization has occurred and has many of us, aside others, assuming that this type of interaction is the norm for Blacks. However, they couldn't be further from the truth. Yelling, cursing, spitting, and fighting should never be accepted as proper ways to engage any type of positive communication for anyone, so why has it become expected for so many African Americans? Can you imagine a projected understanding of what is normal, relating to a living reality of respectful relationships among African American men and women, without society's drama endorsed stereotypes clouding our reflections of one another?

When it comes to situations where people scream and spit profanity like a second language, all should understand that these actions are mainly produced out of habit and can be managed. With the right amount of patience and consideration, all arguments and disagreements can be handled properly, without hurt or painful thoughts of break-ups or divorce.

Disagreements

People are dissimilarly opinionated at times, and that will never change. However, the key to proactively quelling situations that carry the potential of developing into problems is understanding that the diversity of those opinions is not a bad thing. Every disagreement does not have to turn into an argument. It is only the response to disagreeing that takes things to another level. Respectively agreeing to disagree can quickly kill all of that. This is a way of settling differences by mutual concession that people use to create a level playing field when disagreements occur. It is a respectable way of submitting without giving up, but understanding that the other person or group has a valid opinion of their own. This tool can be very useful to those who don't like burning their own bridges. Just think about how good it would be to have a disagreement where neither of the involved parties would take offense to the opinions or suggestions of the other. I call that peace and freedom of mind. Your opinion is always important to you right? From that, you can assume that the other person's opinion is important to them as well. So, when you find yourself in a situation of debate and your way of thinking conflicts with that of someone else's, simply say, "I disagree, but I respect your opinion." If they, in turn, take offense, kindly suggest that they read this passage.

The bottom line is that the person you care about is special and so are you. If, in the future, you and your interest find yourselves headed toward argument, because of a simple disagreement, both of you should realize how special you are to one another and communicate effectively by putting down your anger and letting go of your pride. Learning how to disagree effectively should be done in an effort to keep peace and renounce our human ways of simply messing things up. I know it is hard to do, but who said succeeding was easy?

Arguments

Good relationships are never easy to maintain. That should not be a difficult concept to understand if you know that nothing in life worth fighting for comes easy. There are some things we do, however, that sacrifice the integrity of our relationships; never on purpose, of course. You know the saying, "We frequently hurt the ones we love, because we are around them the most." During those periods where we hurt the ones we love, we allow and use specific forms of communication that present problems and create distance between partners and ourselves. Those types of communication typically spawn from debates, disagreements, and arguments and are most often sparked by something really small and not worth the headache.

Arguing is a natural form of communication, but is often misconstrued and exaggerated, by way of negativity. It almost seems as though yelling and violence, in many circumstances, have replaced the ability of explanation. There are, however, ways to argue effectively and walk away smiling with no love lost.

Here are a few great tips for communicating effectively during disagreements and arguments:

Pay close attention to the subject of the argument. For example, if you and your significant other have conflicting views about where to eat dinner and it turns into, "You always…" or "I'm the one with the good memory," you may have a few issues that need adjustment.

In cases like this, try to avoid bringing up old instances where you thought the other person was wrong or careless. Also, try not to take the difference of opinion as a personal attack on your judgment. Try practicing a little patience and stay away from exaggerated words like never and always. No one always or never does anything, so you can assume that no one would want to hear that.

Take a deep breath and recognize that the person with whom you are arguing is not your enemy, but if you decide to fight, fight fair.

Conflict is a very healthy occurrence in relationships, and if governed correctly, it could be used to strengthen and promote unity within the bond. Control is the key word here. Practice some authentic discipline here and act like the loving, responsible adult you want to be. During the war, try to maximize the positivity in your communication efforts with the goal of fixing or locating the cause of the problem. Take control of your emotions and words, and find a way to reach a common, understood solution by any means. Make it your purpose to make peace and eliminate the distance between you and the person you appreciate. I also suggest that both partners practice speaking to each other in the sweetest way possible, during these times. *Proverbs* (16:24) says: *"Kind words are like honey; sweet to the soul and healthy for the body."* I can promise that, if exercised on both parts without sarcasm and dishonesty, this will work. The charm of sincere and honest words can extinguish the wildest fire. The next time you and your partner bump heads, make sure it brings you closer.

Make sure that what you are arguing over is really what the issue is about.

Many times, arguments are fueled by feelings carried over from other situations or emotions. Usually, when arguments blow up into huge fights, there is more than meets the eye behind the blame. Always remember to be assertive in introspection, and honestly critique your feelings before speaking out in anger. Our emotions sometimes tend to lead our minds away from the issues at hand and that tendency often creates what? That's right! More arguments.

Holding grudges never works.

In order to be a happy person, you cannot walk around with the weight of the world on your shoulders. Negativity kills, so you have to let that stuff go. If someone makes you angry, don't punish your soul by holding it all inside. Use forgiveness as your release and move on, with or without them.

Apologize for hurting someone's feelings, even if you think you did nothing wrong.

The issue here is that everything is not all about you. In some situations, you may feel like you did nothing wrong, but it is the other person who is often left to suffer. Again, put down your pride and express a little sympathy by replying, "I'm sorry you took it that way, but what I meant was etc…" By delivering your message this way, you are showing that you are sympathetic and that you care. Leave pride alone. Trust me! It will consistently get you nowhere but alone.

Stop needing to be right all of the time.

What part of a person's psyche makes them believe that their thoughts are perfect and that the thoughts of others are more than likely incorrect? What is it about being right that causes a person to go 'all in' on their assumptions? What it is called is pride. Just let it go. Your interest in your partner or spouse is worth ten times more than winning a debate. Remember, your spouse is not your enemy, so relax. To be more productive together, we need to start looking further than our own understandings and begin considering and accepting the experiences and opinions of others.

Forgiveness

The undisputed champion of long-lasting relationships is forgiveness. It is a stress free release from the burden of anger and reigns supreme in the court of peace and healing. Used as a tool for sustenance within relationships, this fundamental tool can do wonders for all people.

Unfortunately, anger and frustration, when harbored, both have tendencies to eat away at people. They lead us toward negative thoughts and feelings. Neither one of the two is healthy. The things that are healthy, however, are positive thoughts and actions. You see, negativity and positivity are balanced forces of the universe that exist together; kind of like the Taoist Yin-Yang symbolism which represents the equilibrium of the universe. One cannot touch or control the force of negativity because of its essence; however, one could redirect it. By doing this, a person could cast away, feelings of guilt or hatred that carry great power and bog people down for great periods of time.

By choosing to forgive, you do not accept weakness or stupidity. Your goal is to forgive, but not forget. You do not have to resume any type of relationship with the person who caused you grief, but simply attempt to make your life less stressful by replacing hardened thoughts with positive ones, while continuing to be mindful of the past. It's as simple as that.

Accepting Forgiveness

Pros:

- Gain relief from the hindrance of the past.

- You can dispel pinned feelings of hurt, pain, and anger, while stimulating your healing.

- Forgiveness allows you to liberate yourself no matter what the other person does.

Cons:

- There are none. Just be careful with determining who you should let back in, once you forgive them.

Remember to forgive and not forget. Whether hard times are

brought on by family members, friends, or lovers, we must overcome our pain through forgiveness in order to achieve harmony. You don't have to keep those same people around, but you must lose those bad feelings. Though it may be very difficult to overcome feelings of retribution and finger pointing, try to remember that the power of forgiveness will set you free.

Steps to Forgiveness

1. First, be aware that these steps are not intended to invalidate your feelings or troubles. Confront your pain, apprehension, and resentment and recognize the damage caused.

2. Realize that fear is the entity that comes between success and failure. Also understand that forgiveness can only be grasped after you have eliminated your fear and resentment. Remember that a continuous reliance on anger and resentment will literally destroy your physical health, and cause you great mental anguish.

3. Know that tranquility and peace is what you ultimately want for yourself and your relationship.

4. Consider the fact that forgiveness does not promote weakness, but rather serves as a worthy goal of strength. Forgiveness also does not excuse abuse, the use of negative actions, or any type of harmful behavior.

5. Recognize that you are the master of your fate and the sole controller of your feelings, emotions, and healing.

Forgiveness Exercises For Couples

1. You must both, in a calm and loving manner, agree that you are ready to talk about an issue. Once you are ready to talk, make sure you have an open mind to promote positive communication in an effort to solve your problem.

2. Use fair and equal communication techniques by speaking and listening, and always discuss the concerns you have, toward the issue

or pain caused. The purpose is to understand how you individually feel. Remember to not point fingers or place blame, but try to understand the role of the actions that took place.

3. Whoever accepts responsibility for wrongdoing, whether it is one partner or both, should issue an apology and request forgiveness.

4. The apology and request for forgiveness should be openly acknowledged and respected. After that, the course of action should be determined by the severity of the offense or by the proactive decision made by the offended.

5. Once forgiveness is given, both souls are free, and the paths remain open, whether intertwined or separate, but hopefully together.

We Have to Make It Work

I am a firm believer in the idea that we as a strong people, and as individuals, can achieve anything. That idea also ties over into our relationships. The only thing that truly has any type of control over the success or failure of a relationship is the unified decision of the people involved in the relationship. No matter whether the problem is brought on by busy schedules or long distance interaction, if two people really want to work things out, they will.

In order to welcome a more noticeable and productive life of unity between our men and women, we must ultimately demand the power that it takes to will triumph and achievement into our future. We need each other and we must make things work.

At the end of the day, there are more African American couples than our society cares to acknowledge, who are succeeding happily together. Because of this, we must take the necessary steps to not just understand this truth, but believe in it. Marriage and unity are still the goals, so lets make it happen.

Marriage Is Still the Goal

How do we repair our situation and upgrade our reality for the greater benefits that our future will provide for us? Well, as written previously, starting from our roots would ultimately get us where we need to be by helping us understand the dual importance of a good, solid foundation, along with the significance of the design and creation of that foundation. The roots that I speak of and support refer directly to marriage and family, which both serve as key ingredients to healthy foundations.

In the past, we have reached our most prominent levels when united, but because our marriages and relationships have taken several catastrophic hits over the years, our union has been weakened and many have struggled to grasp that understanding. This, however, brings to mind that old saying, "It takes a village to raise a child." Though true, this statement only scratches the surface. The depth of the truth that fuels this statement openly displays how that same village helps create and sustain the integrity of the family bond. It is vital that you and I understand the importance of community and how the affect of its power can resonate through our daily living like the ring from the bell of freedom Dr. King prayed for.

Additionally, the situation we are in has forced me to search for an outside understanding of the decline in our relational status. What I have found has astounded me and often leaves me thinking, "I knew this, but didn't pay it much attention." My finding has allowed me to glance deeper into the eye of American progression and see how the traditional direction of notably significant institutions such as church and school has been disputed and redirected by society's destructive vehicles like media and other politically driven and administered forms of education and information delivery. Both bring very important tools for gain and personal achievement for all people.

So, my message to all of my beloved readers is to take time to realize how important both a solid understanding and a clear mind are, in all efforts to support our reparation.

Yes, marriage is still the ultimate goal, but a few things need to happen before we even attempt to take steps toward that goal individually.

1. The overall level of mutual disgust among Black men and women is horrendous. Again, this is something that we did not create on our own, but it is something that only we can fix. This can be done by exercising forgiveness and by increasing our levels of positivity and intelligent dating selection strategies. Our trust must return and we must forgive to move forward.

2. The games must stop. Lies, deception and mental abuse are all

tools exploited by both men and women, but if those men and women saw the importance of trust being more beneficial than that of deception, then our optimistic views would automatically work to empower the minds of others in an effort to keep those evil tools removed and isolated.

3. We must strengthen our encompassing levels of faith within ourselves as well as with one another, because without faith, there is no purpose, and without purpose, there is nothing.

I'll say it again, "Marriage is still the goal," and despite all of the rumors, stereotypes, and hard times, marriage and family life among African Americans is alive and flourishing. The numbers and statistics may not paint a pretty picture in the minds of many, but our situations are improving daily. The rate of marriages within our cultural circle is rising and I am extremely happy about that. In light of this, I can't place enough emphasis on the importance of family and the power of faith. So with that in mind, let us now set the example for the rest of America to abide by. After all, we are notably the most imitated, yet most feared ethnic group in America, so why not give it a shot. Wouldn't it feel good to look back and say, "I made that happen?"

Twelve

A Final Word

"Our deepest fear is not that we are inadequate. Our deepest fear is that we are powerful beyond measure... As we are liberated from our own fear, our presence automatically liberates others."

Marianne Williamson

Acknowledgment and appreciation are acts that everyone likes to receive from others. Together, they form the ingredients of the social aspects of human nature, which individually contribute to the satisfaction of the human psyche. Unfortunately, the recurring issues that come to mind when focusing on principles like these bring light to the way people point out negative circumstances that men sometimes bring about, more than showing appreciation for the positive situations that those men consistently create.

Because of the exaggerated stereotyping of the majority of Black men, many carry much doubt and stand hopeless. Ironically, the ones who dwell in skepticism the most, happen to be Black men. This makes it tougher for our leaders and kings to thrive, because not only do they have to deal with their own particular questions of the validity of their existences and roles, they have to live knowing that a massive group of their women are also participating in these acts of dubiosity. What worse way is there to live for a man? This is why we must not bash or demean them, but help them gain a more positive and progressive understanding of who they are and who they can grow to be. Our men are kings and they need to be reminded of that in an increasingly repetitive fashion. After all, how can our men love themselves without knowing their identity.

As a good Black man, I have realized a few things in life. One is that it feels very lonely when people don't believe in you or what you do. More importantly, not receiving acknowledgement, praise, or any type of acclaim for the things I have done as one of the good guys has made me feel less important at times. However, I have come to learn, again, that this has been done by design, and it is not necessarily our fault. I am not speaking of some extra type of ego stroking. I am simply referring to a simple, every so often, "You are a good man, and I appreciate you," for our men who deserve it.

Our mindsets were placed in such a way that made our overall senses of appreciation for each other lay dormant, below radar. Therefore, our levels of recognition would not pick up on the important aspects of mutual gratification, especially toward our men. So when left abandoned and feeling unimportant, what do men do? We goof off and act like there is nothing to fight for. We act as though there is no reason to justify our honor. That is why displayed appreciation for our kings is so crucial. If we don't believe in them, then what should they fight for?

Trying to help out as much as I can, I make it a point to constantly revise my individual roles and goals as an African American man, within my community. Because I love my people, I have taken on a role to openly praise Black men who have made an impact on my life. I let them know that they deserve proper respect and recognition. From family men who take care of their wives and children, to single fathers who I meet on the street, struggling with raising their kids by themselves, "I admire and salute you." From men who are dedicated to their careers, to men who work relentlessly at their relationships with women, "I praise your existence."

Last but never least, I cannot forget to show my love and gratitude to the women and men who show Black men nothing but support. You inspire me, because you do what others choose not to, in the name of goodness. Thank you to those who use their power to enlighten the world with the Black man's truth and legend.

Thank you to everyone who makes an effort to help. Many thanks to Raheem Devaughn for demanding the belief that we Black men need, loud enough for the ears and minds of millions. I am also thankful for Heather Headly for not being afraid to sing about the man she desires. I appreciate Jill Scott so much for suggesting that we take those long walks, while telling me why she needs me. I am always glad to hear that. "I need you too Sista, and I am not stopping until I get to you." Much love and respect to my brother from another, Will Smith, for being such a positive a role model, for Black men and boys everywhere. Andre from Outkast, Stank you very much. You are something else Brotha. Peace and love to my hero, the good Rev. Dr. Martin Luther King. I appreciate and love you. Dr. Maya Angelou. You are my She-ro. Many thanks also go out to Anthony Hamilton. I am still proud of you, and remain inspired. Finally, I have to give a very special thanks to Angie Stone. You are truly my soul sister. After all, who else writes songs about me and my brothers, while promoting my existence and the reign of my dominion? I cannot tell you how much you have influenced me. Please continue to help us understand our worth and glory.

To all who lead and follow, I uplift you and your effort for our men. My only regret is that I cannot ask you to help enough.

One More Thing

Be strong, beloved, and allow God's will to overcome your own and guide you to a greater sense of righteousness. We are a strong people, but stronger united. Please be forthright in creating a productive understanding for yourself, others, and those of future generations. We shall overcome the oppression that still lives, being nourished by the hatred of others. However, we must first deal with the demons that infect our very being. It is essential for us to realize that within ourselves, lay habits and tendencies that blind our judgment and lead us down hindering paths. From that realization, a connection must be made to deliver you and I to a place that forces us to have better appreciation for what is ultimately imperative for the good of Black men, women, and children.

From this day forth, try not to think about what someone can do for you and your situation. Make a stronger attempt to enforce your sense of appreciation and care for others. That is one of the surest ways we will get anywhere, brothers and sisters. Women must grasp the situation of men from both sides of the fence and know that good men are alive and well. Men must also step into the shoes of women and understand the pain within their hearts.

Unified, we will arrive at that mountaintop that awaits our landing, and together we will bask in the glory of our strengths. However, we must first put down our pride long enough to take a long glance in the mirror and face our demons. Now is the time for us to fight our habitually lobotomized ways of thinking and honor the love and presence of our men and women; for we honor God by doing so.

I love you, and I will do whatever is necessary to protect and preserve our love for each other. Peace and blessings.

Your Brother,
Your Son,
Your Friend

Aaron Anwar Smith

The Beginning...

References

Anderson, Claude, ED.D. *Powernomics: The National Plan To Empower Black America.* Maryland: Powernomics Corporation of America, Inc. 2001.

Cokeley, Christopher J, Blake., and Aaron M. *Why Can't You See Me? Good Men Do Exist!*. Love Life Publishing, LLC, 2003.

Freeman, Joel A., and Griffin, Don B. *Return To Glory: The Powerful Stirring of the Black Race*. Pennsylvania: Destiny Image Publishers, Inc., 2003.

Jackson, Chris. *The Black Christian Singles Guide To Dating And Sexuality*. Michigan: Zondervan Publishing House, 1999.

McGraw, Phillip C. PH.D. *Relationship Rescue*. New York: Hyperion, 2000.

Richard B. Moore. *The Name Negro Its Origin and Evil Use*. Baltimore: Black Classic Press, 1960.

Woodson, Carter G. *The Miseducation of The Negro*. Washington, DC: The Associated Publishers, Inc, 1990.

Randolph, Laura B. "Four Things Black Women Say They Wish Black Men Knew." Ebony. July, 1991.

"Negro." Wikipedia. http://en.wikipedia.org/wiki/Negro (5 Feb 2007).

"African American." Wikipedia. http://en.wikipedia.org/wiki/African_American (5 Feb 2007).

"Black People." http://en.wikipedia.org/wiki/Black_people (5 Feb 2007)

Kinnon, Joy Bennett "The shocking state of Black marriage: experts say many will never get married". Ebony. Nov 2003. FindArticles.com. 19 Jul. 2007. http://findarticles.com/p/articles/mi_m1077/is_1_59/ai_110361377